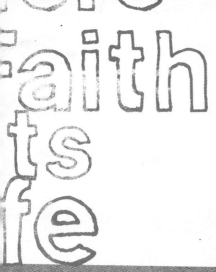

Where
Faith
Meets
Real Life

a teen study of james

by andrew phillips

21st Century Christian

Table of Contents

Table of Contents

1. Everybody Hurts   7

2. Tempted and Tried   15

3. Don't Just Stand There,
    Do Something!   21

4. Playing Favorites   27

5. Your Faith—Dead or Alive?   33

6. Taming the Tongue   39

7. Wise Up   45

8. Friend or Enemy?   53

9. Humble Yourself   59

10. Life is Short   65

11. Rich & Famous...
    and About to Be Miserable   71

12. Hold On!   79

13. Our Most Powerful Weapon   85

    Leader's Guide Pages   91

Dedication

This book is dedicated to my wife Kathryn, whose love and patience made it possible for me to work on this project, and to Luke, whose arrival reminded me how important it is to make God's Word come alive for the next generation.

A Word to the Teacher

First of all, thank you for taking the time and effort to teach the Bible. I am convinced there is no better way to spend our time than studying and teaching God's life-changing Word. This book is designed to be an aid in outlining class sessions and keeping students focused on the text. You will probably want to consult a good commentary or Bible dictionary for background information on James, the half-brother of Christ, and the readers he is addressing. While those facts are important, these lessons will focus primarily on the practical aspect of the book as it applies to the lives of teenagers.

Each lesson is intended to cover a specific section of verses. There will be more information, options, and activities than you will have time for in a single class session. It is always better to have more material than needed than get done with a lesson and realize there is still time left! Don't worry about covering every single one; pick and choose which activities fit your class and your context. Be sure to use at least one or two of the "Time-Outs," since they are designed to appeal to the various learning styles in your class. Above all, pray about it and be creative. If something written here gives you a better idea to use in your class, go for it! No one knows your students better than you, and you are the best judge as to what will be effective. My prayer is that God will bless all of us as we teach His Word!

.

Chapter 1

Everybody Hurts

James 1:1-12

At the age of 27, Aron Ralston loved rock-climbing. He didn't just love it; he was good at it. One day in April of 2003, he set out for a routine climb. He didn't bother to tell any of his friends where he would be climbing that day; he just threw his supplies into his truck and headed for the site. As he was climbing, he reached a boulder that had become wedged into a tight mountain crevice. When he crossed the 800 pound boulder, it suddenly moved, pinning his right hand against a rock wall. In his book *Between a Rock and a Hard Place*, Aron vividly describes the moment he realized there was no easy way to escape. The boulder had trapped him in a desolate area more than 8 miles from his truck. He eventually *amputated his right arm with a pocket knife* in order to free himself. For Aron, the pain of cutting his arm was terrible, but it was worth it to preserve his life. Sometimes life is like that – in order for something good to happen, we have to experience pain.

It doesn't matter who you are, where you live, or how much money you make – you are going to hurt. Somewhere along the way, a friend is going to turn his back on you, a family member will suddenly become ill, the person you planned to marry will say you aren't the one, and you will be dealing with serious pain. No one gets to live a pain-free life. You can't make enough money to avoid pain; if you could, no millionaire would ever file for bankruptcy. You can't gain enough popularity to avoid pain; if you could, then no movie star or pop singer would ever develop a drug addiction or eating disorder. You can't build up enough muscle to avoid pain; if you could, then no professional athlete would ever get caught up in a scandal or dragged into court. The bottom line is we are all going to hurt. Here is the important question: how will we handle it?

Pain Is...Good?

Have you read about all those people in the Bible who had leprosy? Found several times in the Bible, the term "leprosy" refers to a terrible, incurable skin condition. The main condition is known as "Hansen's Disease" today, and we have developed some effective ways to treat it. Those treatments were not available in Bible times, and a person would often not even realize he or she had leprosy until the disease was in an advanced stage. While there are several different symptoms of this skin disease, one is a loss of sensation in the skin. That means that a person with leprosy might not feel anything he or she touched.

Sounds great, right? No pain! You would never have to feel heat when you touched a plate that was too hot. You would never have to wear gloves when you made a snowball. You would never have to shout when someone stepped on your toe. Life would be great without pain, wouldn't it? Actually, this characteristic is one of the worst symptoms of leprosy. When this numbness sets in, you can burn yourself without knowing it. You can cut yourself and begin bleeding profusely before it catches your eye. You can break bones or damage muscles without realizing it. When we hear horror stories about people with leprosy whose skin and appendages began to fall off, we know that this lack of sensation is partly to blame. If you feel no pain, you may not notice a serious problem with your body until it is too late.

So what does any of this have to do with James? James begins his letter with a discussion of pain and suffering. In fact, he dives right into that topic with the second verse of chapter one, telling his readers they should consider it a joy to experience trials. In other words, they should get excited about suffering. At first that doesn't seem to make much sense. After all, if you saw someone who was excited because tragedy had struck his family, what would you think? Although it might sound strange at first, James gives us a clear explanation of why suffering should give us joy.

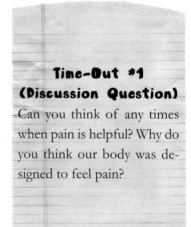

Time-Out #1 (Discussion Question)

Can you think of any times when pain is helpful? Why do you think our body was designed to feel pain?

What Do You Get?

First of all, suffering develops perseverance. You've probably heard someone say, "Whatever doesn't kill you just makes you stronger." The first reason James tells us to rejoice is because the more we suffer, the more perseverance we'll develop. He writes, "Consider it pure joy, my brothers, whenever you face trials of many kinds, because you know the testing of your faith develops perseverance" (1:2). The word "perseverance" refers to the ability someone has to endure difficult times and stay faithful to God. To help us understand this term better, let's look at an example James uses. Later on in the book, James points to Job's perseverance, stating "As you know, we consider blessed those who have persevered. You have heard of Job's perseverance and seen what the Lord finally brought about. The Lord is full of compassion and mercy" (5:11).

James is reminding his readers of Job, a man who lived many years earlier and whose story is recorded in the Old Testament. Job displays incredible perseverance, because he was a good man who lost almost everything. His flocks and herds were killed, which meant more than just the death of a few animals. In Job's day, wealth was often measured by livestock, so Job lost a great deal of wealth. He lost all his children and began to experience painful sores all over his body. His wife told him to "curse God and die" and his three friends (Eliphaz, Bildad, and Zophar) told Job he was being punished for sins he had committed. When we read the book of Job, however, we find out that Job had not sinned. In fact, just the opposite is true; following God made Job one of Satan's targets.

The reason James mentions Job's story is because of its ending. If you read the conclusion of the book, God rewards Job, making him well and giving him more livestock and more children. At the end of his life, Job is wealthier than he was at the beginning. Job reminds us that all those who follow God will suffer, and sometimes it will be for no good reason. The only reason Job experienced all this tragedy is because Satan attacked him, believing that if Job lost all he had, he would turn his back on God. Of course, Job didn't know this. All he knew was that life was unfair. After all, he was a model believer. Why should he suffer? He was not always patient with God, but he stuck it out. He persevered. We aren't always going to understand every reason behind the trials we face, but we need to follow Job's example. Every trial gives us another chance to develop perseverance.

10

Think about it this way – picture the practice of weight-lifting. The actual act of lifting weights causes trauma (or stress) to the muscles. After the lifting is completed, the muscles react to that trauma by growing back larger and stronger. In a couple of days, when a person lifts weights again, the process repeats itself. Like a broken bone that grows back stronger once the fracture has healed, muscles become stronger only when they have experienced the stress of working hard.

Grow Up

Perseverance helps us become complete. James uses the word "perfect" in verse 4, but when he used the term, it meant something different than our modern definition. When we think of someone who is perfect, we picture an individual without any faults who never makes a mistake. That is not what James is saying. The biblical meaning of that term is "complete." When someone has reached "perfection," they have been completed. James isn't telling us that perseverance will make us into Super-Christians that never make mistakes; he is letting us know that if we want to become "complete" people who have everything we need, we must develop perse-

Time-Out #2 (Activity)

Watch your teacher (or a volunteer) try to lift a heavy weight. How did that person do? Was he/she able to lift it quite a few times?

Imagine you had never lifted a weight in your life, and you walked up to a 500 pound barbell and tried to lift it. What would happen? The only way to lift a weight that heavy is to train your muscles. In the same way, the difficulties we face in life are preparation for us. This year's problems help us develop the perseverance we will need for next year's challenges. Imagine living for years without experiencing pain and then being hit with a terrible tragedy, completely unprepared. It would be a little bit like trying to lift that 500 pound weight when you have never worked out in your life. As He helps us, God is able to use the trials we face to prepare us to handle tests further down the road. Our challenges will often be unfair, and they won't make any sense to us. Our job is to persevere – to trust in God no matter what. One day, when we face an overwhelming challenge, we will be thankful that God helped us develop perseverance.

verance. The word "mature" comes from this idea, too. Has anyone ever told you to "grow up!"? James is telling us that we can't do that without perseverance.

But what if we aren't complete? If we don't have wisdom, James tells us we can ask God for it. Wisdom is one of the most important things we can ever obtain. The Old Testament book of Proverbs tells us repeatedly that we need to strive after wisdom. Proverbs 4:5 states, "Get wisdom! Get understanding! Do not forget, nor turn away from the words of my mouth." Verse 7 goes on to say, "Wisdom is the principal thing; therefore get wisdom." In fact, that entire book is filled with wise sayings for Christian living. Our entire lives should be spent in an effort to get more wisdom.

James does tell us a specific way to approach God in prayer – with faith and without doubting. The writer of Hebrews describes faith as being certain of what is hoped for and sure of what is not seen (11:1). Prayer really is an exercise of faith; we cannot see God, yet we should make sure when praying that we are sure of what we do not see. James also calls us to ask without doubting, which can often be difficult, since we all struggle with doubt from time to time. When we find ourselves questioning God's power, we do feel like a "wave of the sea, driven by the wind." We don't want to be that double-minded man James mentions, who asks God for blessings even though he doesn't expect

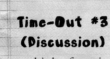

Time-Out #3 (Discussion)

Can you think of a painful experience in your life that helped you handle another challenge down the road?

Time-Out #4 (Discussion)

Read through the following Psalms of David: Psalm 13, Psalm 22. Does it comfort you to know that other biblical figures like David struggled with doubt? These psalms move from doubting frustration to awed faithfulness. Repeating them to ourselves can help us move from doubt to trust. What passages of Scripture can you memorize and repeat to yourself when you are faced with doubts?

anything in return. But, we still have to admit that every Christian, at one point or another, struggles with doubt. This is a time when we truly know the power of God's Word, since the Bible shows us followers of God who struggled with doubt.

The Ultimate Headgear

Perseverance allows Christians to receive a "crown of life." Have you noticed how positive James has been throughout these verses? He's talked about difficult issues, using words like "trials" and "suffering," but he keeps saying things like "Consider it joy" and "Blessed is a man who perseveres under trial." Have you ever noticed how two people can look at the same object and see totally different things? You and I might look at a tragedy as a terrible life experience, but James sees those times as joyful blessings. In verse 1, James reveals that he intends for this letter to go to Christians abroad, many of whom seem to be suffering for various reasons. In verse 9, James describes rich and poor people in a completely different way – he tells us that poor people have a high position, while rich people have a low position.

Jesus made similar statements when He walked the earth; He often found more faith with sinners and tax collectors than He did with the wealthy and influential teachers. For example, Mark 10:17-31 recalls a man who ran up to Jesus and knelt before Him, asking what he should do to gain eternal life. When Jesus lists the commandments from the Law of Moses, the man claims to have kept those since he was a boy. This man (often referred to as the "Rich Young Ruler," based on this passage and similar ones in Matthew and Luke) seems to have a high position. After all, he has kept all the commandments. He was willing to run up to Jesus and kneel at His feet, a display which was certainly embarrassing for a prestigious man. When Jesus asked him to give up those riches, however, that man could not part with his wealth. Jesus responded by saying it was hard for rich people to enter the kingdom of Heaven (vss. 24, 25). Jesus' statement shocked His followers, since many people viewed riches as a sign of God's blessings. In other words, the richer you were, the more blessed by God you were. If you were blessed greatly, you must be a good person.

Both Jesus and James tell us something different, though. Jesus concludes His discussion by stating, "Many who are first will be last, and the last, first." James paints the same picture in verses 10 and 11, depicting rich men who pass away in the middle of their pursuit of wealth. Just as Jesus said the kingdom is only accessible if we give up the idol of wealth, James tells us that the crown of life is available only when we have persevered under trial. Our trials will be different than those faced by James' original readers, but the source of our perseverance remains the same.

Time-Out #5 (Discussion)

Bring in a glass of water, and fill it up halfway. Ask the age-old question – is the glass half-full or half-empty? Also, consider the famous visual illusion popularized by British cartoonist W.E. Hill. (Do an internet search for "visual illusion W.E. Hill.") Do you see a young woman or an old lady? Depending on which one you look for, your perspective changes. The same is true when we handle tragedy; what we look for determines how we view what happens to us.

Putting It All Together

1. How does James view trials? Are there ways his view of trials can help us live more fulfilling lives?

2. What three things do we gain by persevering? Can you think of some biblical examples of perseverance?

3. Have you thought of a quality you lack for which you can begin praying?

4. In what ways does our culture promote the pursuit of wealth rather than perseverance? Brainstorm specific examples.

5. Make a brief list of the trials Christians face today. In what ways are the trials we experience different than the ones James would have known? How are they similar?

Taking It Home

This week, keep a piece of paper in your pocket as you go to school, practice, Bible class, etc. Write down the different challenges you face on a daily basis. Pray for strength to handle those difficulties, and try to think of ways you can learn from them.

Chapter 2

Tempted and Tried
James 1:13-18

My wife Kathryn teaches elementary school, and every year she reads the book *Where the Red Fern Grows* to her class. In it, Wilson Rawls writes about a boy named Billy who wants to be a great hunter. He buys two puppies, but before he can train them to be hunting dogs, he must catch a raccoon. His grandfather gives him some advice on setting a raccoon trap. Billy takes a brace and a bit, making a hole just large enough for a racoon's hand to slip inside. Billy put a shiny piece of tin on the bottom, and waited. Eventually, a raccoon came along that was so excited about the piece of tin, he shoved his arm into the trap. He wrapped his fist around the tin, but when he tried to pull his arm out, he couldn't. The only way to escape from the trap was to let go of the piece of tin, but the raccoon was too stubborn to drop it.

That story provides a great picture of temptation, doesn't it? The piece of tin wasn't worth much (especially not worth dying for), but the raccoon wasn't thinking about that. All he could see was how shiny it was, and all he knew was that he wanted it. Satan presents sin that way for us. He makes it look exciting and fulfilling, when it will only leave us weak and vulnerable. James may have lived a long time ago, but not much about sin and temptation has changed since then. Satan still uses the same tactics, and James' strategy will still work.

How to Handle Temptation

First—Realize the Source

James makes it crystal clear that temptation is the work of Satan, not of God. Satan has been at work tempting human beings since the Garden of Eden, and no one gets a free pass. Everyone is tempted. Even Jesus, after He was baptized by John, was led out in the wilderness and tempted. Satan, the source of temptation, attacks Jesus directly. Notice what happens when Jesus is tempted – He quotes Scripture. You see, Satan is the source of temptation, but God is the source of strength to handle temptation. Open up to Matthew 4, and notice how Jesus teaches us that fact.

In Matthew 4:4, immediately after Satan challenged Jesus to turn the stones around Him into bread (Jesus had fasted for 40 days and would have been incredibly hungry), Jesus responds by quoting Moses' words in Deuteronomy 8:3. Jesus knew the source of temptation, and He also knew the source of strength when tempted – dependence on the Word of God. This doesn't mean we should just memorize the words of Scripture. We have to understand what those words mean and apply them in our lives. In verse 6, Satan quotes Scripture during one of his temptations. Sometimes, the temptations we face can look right, feel good, and even sound scriptural. We have to understand Scripture in order to know when it is being used correctly and when it isn't. Jesus was able to respond to Satan's attack with a full understanding of God's Word. We not only need to learn Scripture, we need to make sure we understand and apply it.

Time-Out #1 (Group Activity)

Divide up into three groups, and search the Bible for passages to help you combat temptation. One group will look for Scriptures that teach, one group will look for Scriptures that encourage, and the third group will look for Scriptures that remind us of Heaven. Then, compare notes. Once a list has been formed, everyone should write down these passages and take them home. Keep that list with you, and when you are challenged by the source of temptation, look to the source of strength. Remember, it is important to commit the words of the Bible to memory, but we also need to understand and act on them.

Second—Understand the Process

If we want to overcome temptation, we have to *understand the process*. James maps it out for us in verses 14 and 15:

Step#1 – Our own lust draws us away from God. We can see this happening when we start compromising our beliefs to rationalize a certain action. We start dating someone we really like, and we immediately begin rationalizing how far we can take the physical relationship. We think, "But we really love each other," or "A lot of other couples I know do that, so it can't be a big deal." It is amazing what we can rationalize when we want something badly enough.

Step #2 – Lust gives birth to sin. Once our lust has drawn us away from God and convinces us to rationalize our actions, we carry it out and wind up in the grip of sin. It is important for each of us to realize that a sin I commit is almost always the result of a lust I have let develop. We don't just sin out of nowhere; we sin because we allow lust to grow in our lives unchecked.

Step #3 – Sin brings about death. The word "death" in the Bible means something more than the current definition. "Death" always indicates "separation." Physical death is the separation of a soul from a physical body. Spiritual death is the separation of a soul from God. When sin creeps into our lives, it does just that – it separates us from God. The ultimate result of that separation (if we don't do anything about it) is death – both physical and spiritual.

This process is easy to see in the life of David, the Old Testament king. What was his most well-known sin? Adultery. Even if you haven't read much of the Bible, you have probably heard of David and Bathsheba. Where did that sin begin? When we read 2 Samuel 11, we immediately see where the whole process started. Read verses 1-5; Bathsheba isn't summoned to David's palace until verse 4, but David begins walking down the path to sin in verse 3. While the other kings were out in battle, David (who was a brave warrior) decided to stay home. That night, he walked around the roof (have you ever noticed that temptations grow stronger at night?), and he saw a beautiful woman. Now, up until this point, David had not sinned. He saw a beautiful woman bathing, and he could have just looked away and let it go at that. But, in verse 3, we see step #1 of the temptation process: David inquires about her.

David encountered a physical temptation, and he let lust drag him further into it. Rather than turning away, he pursued this lust by asking about her. One of David's servants told David the identity of this mystery woman – she was the wife of one of his best soldiers. David sent for her anyway. Why? David allowed lust to drag him away, and once we are in the grip of lust, it is hard for us to listen to reason. Have you ever noticed that when you are faced with lust, it is hard to think straight? Once we've been drawn away from God's plan, the weakness of our flesh takes over, and it is almost impossible to talk ourselves into doing what is right. That's why decisions must be made before we encounter temptation. The time to decide to stay pure until marriage is not when you are alone with your girlfriend/boyfriend; it is before you are ever in that situation. The time to decide not to get drunk is not when you are offered a beer by one of your friends; it is before that ever happens. In Job 31:1, Job states, "I have made a covenant with my eyes. How then could I gaze at a virgin?" Job made a decision not to lust before he faced temptation. Here, David does just the opposite. Ultimately, this act leads to step #2 – the sin of adultery. That sin leads to death (step #3) – the physical death of Uriah, as well as David and Bathsheba's child, and the spiritual separation of David from God, for which David later asks for forgiveness.

Time-Out #2 (Question)

Brainstorm a few of the most common sins that affect teenagers. You might see kids at school, or even good friends, struggle with these temptations. Try to work through the process James lays out for us. Write on the board:

Step #1 – What lust draws people away and gives birth to this sin?

Step #2 – Once this sin becomes reality, what effect does it have?

Now, try to think of ways to be proactive and head off this sin at step #1. How can you prevent lust from dragging you away?

Third—Lean On God

Notice the way James describes God; he states that with God there is "no variation or shifting shadow." In other words, God will remain a steady, stable support for those who lean on Him. This is important to remember, because all people we know – our parents, our relatives, and our friends – are imperfect. Some time in life, they will let us down. Even worse, at some point, we will let them down. The writer of Hebrews understood this, writing "Jesus Christ is the same yesterday, today, and forever," (Hebrews 13:8). The writer goes on to urge readers not to be "carried away" by strange teachings. Our world is filled with teachings which don't glorify or honor God. Almost every time we flip through a magazine or check out the internet, we are exposed to individuals who do not honor God with their lives. As Christians, we shouldn't be carried away by that. We can't lean on celebrities, musicians, or the popular kids at school for support. True, lasting support for our lives will only come from God.

Did you notice that *every good and perfect gift* is from above? All of our blessings came from God; if we have something good, it is only because of Him. If you have a house to live in, food to eat, or money to spend, it is only because of God. You might have studied hard to earn good grades, but your mind came from God. You might have worked hard to make extra money, but your strength came from God. You might have practiced hard to excel in sports, but your ability came from God. No matter what our blessings are, they didn't come from us. Once we realize that, we can know how important it is to follow God and listen only to Him.

Putting It All Together

1. What is the source of our temptations? Does God ever tempt us?

Time-Out #3 (Activity)

Choose a volunteer, and ask them to walk across the room blindfolded. While that person is trying to make it across, call out to them with wrong directions. It doesn't matter where you tell them to go, just as long as it isn't the right way. After that person finally makes it across (if that happens), try it again. This time, everyone will shout wrong directions, except for one person. This individual will walk beside the blindfolded volunteer, telling them the way in a soft voice. After the second time across, ask the blindfolded volunteer these questions: What was it like to walk through the maze with the wrong directions? How did it feel to try following the correct directions through all the noise?

Now, think about life for a minute. How many temptations come at us from all directions every day and push us off track? We have to listen hard for the still, small voice of God to lead us in the right direction. We also have to realize that the voices of others may lead us in the wrong direction. Only by listening to God's voice can we make it through the challenges of life.

2.   In what ways does Satan tempt you today? What Scriptures have you studied in this class session that you can remember when you face those temptations?

3.   Think about times when you have experienced the temptation process James mentioned (you don't have to share it with anyone, just think about it). Keep those times in mind the next time you face a temptation.

4.   Can you believe that David, a man after God's own heart, would struggle with such terrible sins? How does that make you feel about your own temptations?

5.   What are some of the "good and perfect gifts" God has given you?

Taking It Home

Put that list of Scriptures you made in a place where you see it often – like your locker or closet door. Keep it there as a reminder of some tools God has given you to fight temptation.

Chapter 3

Don't Just Stand There, Do Something!
James 1:19-27

Do you think most people in today's world believe in what the Bible says? Check out these figures from recent surveys:

80% of Americans refer to themselves as Christians.

Only 38% have attended a worship service in the past 7 days.

12% of Americans read the Bible every day.

Isn't that interesting? 80% of Americans call themselves Christians, but only 38% of them attend a worship service regularly, and only 12% read their Bible every day. Saying you believe in something is one thing, but acting on that belief is another thing entirely. James gives us an important challenge in these verses – it is not enough just to listen to God's Word, we have to act on what we believe.

Listen Up

In verse 19, we are commanded to be quick to listen but slow to speak and slow to become angry. If you were to keep a count during the day of how much time you listen and how much time you talk, which activity would log the most minutes? An old expression states that since God gave us two ears and one mouth, we should try to listen twice as much as we speak. That's hard, isn't it? When you hear something you disagree with, don't you want to speak up right then and there? When a friend talks to other people about you behind your back, don't you want to yell at them immediately?

This might be our human nature, but it is not God's nature. He tells us to be slow to speak and slow to anger, since man's anger does not produce God's righteousness. Notice, James is writing about man's anger, not God's. There is such a thing as righteous anger, like the kind Jesus displayed when He cleared the money-changers out of the temple (John 2:13-17). The Jews had turned God's temple into a money-making machine, and Jesus demanded that they stop. Most of the time, though, our anger isn't the righteous anger Jesus displayed about a serious problem that needed to be addressed. It is usually a selfish anger that focuses on making ourselves feel better. That can lead us to saying things to our friends that we don't mean or doing things to other youth group members that we will later regret. If we can just remember to stop and listen before we rush to say something, we can avoid the hurt feelings and damaged relationships that come with being quick to speak and quick to become angry.

Learn God's Word

James tells us in verse 21 to put away our "filthiness." He chose a term that often referred to dirty clothes or even earwax! He reminds us how gross and disgusting the filth of sin can be. In its place, God wants us to receive His Word. The order here is important; before God's Word can have its effect in our lives, we must put away our own filthiness. Paul refers to this process as the "old self" that is put to death when we become Christians (Romans 6:6; Ephesians 4:22). In other words, following God's will require a lifestyle change. We have to let go of our old selves in order to begin our new life with God.

We also need humility if we want God's Word to have its effect on us. Have you ever known someone who *always* had to be right? It didn't matter

Time-Out #1

Can you think of a time when someone said or did something to you because of anger? How did that make you feel? Now, think of a time in which you said or did something to someone else because you were angry. Don't you think that person(s) felt the same way?

Picture the person who said or did something mean to you out of anger. Put yourself in his or her place. What caused that individual to say or do those things? If you haven't already, pray that God will help you forgive that person. If you see that person often, go tell that individual that you have forgiven him or her.

Now, think back to that time you said or did something to someone else out of anger. Did you ever apologize and ask to be forgiven? If not, maybe you can take care of that this week. Pray that God will help you to overcome anger in the future.

what the argument, this individual determined to come out on top. We can't have that kind of attitude and follow God's Word, because submitting to His will requires us to admit when we have messed up and do something about it. The more we read in God's Word, the more we realize our own imperfections, and the more we can appreciate God's forgiveness and guidance.

Live God's Way

How much time do you spend in front of the mirror each day? Can you imagine ever leaving home without checking yourself in the mirror to see how you look? We live in an image-conscious society that places a great deal of emphasis on our physical selves. We take showers, comb our hair, stress over what we will wear that day and whether or not our face has broken out during the night. We use mirrors to help us prepare and look our best. If we see that our hair is messed up or we have something in our teeth, we use mirrors to help us take care of the situation.

In verses 23-25, James uses that image to describe how we improve our spiritual lives. He compares someone who hears the Word without obeying it to someone who looks in a mirror and immediately walks away, forgetting his reflection. Can you picture someone who looks into a mirror and sees that his hair is messed up, his nose is running, his

Time-Out #2

Can you think of a few lifestyle changes that have to be made when someone becomes a Christian? As a class, list as many of those changes as you can imagine.

In verse 21, James reminds us that the Word of God can save our souls. In August of 2007, Brendon Schweigert, a young soldier stationed in Iraq, was attempting to retrieve a tank when a sniper shot him. The bullet hit a small Bible he carried with him in his shirt pocket. Had it not hit the Bible, it likely would have ricocheted off the edge of his bullet-proof vest and gone into his chest. For Brendon, the Bible saved his physical life. In order for God's Word to save our spiritual lives, however, we will have to do more than carry it around in our pocket. James will go on in this chapter to encourage Christians not to be "hearers only," but to take action on what God's Word teaches. Before we can do that, we have to know His Word.

24

Time-Out #3

Check out the following ways to help you spend time in God's Word:

You might want to use a resource like the *One-Year Bible* to help you make it through the entire Bible in one year.

The book of Proverbs has 31 chapters, and each month has 30-31 days (except February). Try reading the chapter of Proverbs that corresponds with each day – you will read through the entire book each month, and you will gain some incredible wisdom!

We all spend time on a school bus or waiting in traffic. Why not try listening to the Bible on your cd or mp3 player while you are riding to school or heading to work?

Try keeping a journal by your Bible and recording your thoughts as you read Scriptures. Ask questions like, "How does this passage change the way I should live?" or "What can I learn about God from this chapter?" Take a look through your notes every so often to remind yourself what you have learned.

You could invest in some study resources, like a good commentary or Bible dictionary. These can be especially helpful for some of the more difficult books like Ezekiel or Revelation. Be sure to pay more attention to the facts in those resources (locations of biblical places, word meanings, etc.) than the author's thoughts. No commentary is perfect – the Bible is our ultimate guide.

clothes are way too big and his shoes are mismatched, then walking away without doing anything? It seems crazy doesn't it? It is even crazier to look into God's Word, realize we need to live differently, and then do nothing about it.

Have you ever known someone who went to worship services, devotionals, and youth rallies, sang the songs, listened to the lessons, yet never really changed? Has that ever described you? In verse 25, James describes someone who "looks intently at the perfect law of liberty," which describes God's Word. This phrase actually indicates someone who looks closely in order to change his appearance. We have to look closely at God's Word in order to change our lives. Verses 26 and 27 show us that a Christian life includes actively watching what we say (we'll discuss that subject in more detail a little bit later), visiting orphans and widows, and keeping ourselves unspotted by the world. Those kinds of actions require intentional effort on our part, and we need to be examining ourselves continually to see if we are putting forth that effort. If we think it is important to spend time in front of a physical mirror, isn't it that much more important to spend time in front of a spiritual one?

Putting It All Together

1. Have you ever known someone who was a good listener? What kind of qualities did they display? Maybe we can use some of those qualities in our efforts to do more listening and less talking.

2. Is it always wrong to be angry? Why or why not?

3. James tells us that we will be blessed if we are doers of the Word and not forgetful hearers (verse 25). Brainstorm some ways that God blesses those who do His Word.

4. Is it possible for someone's religion to be worthless? How?

5. Verse 27 shows us how important it is to care for widows and orphans. What are some ways you and your youth group can accomplish that mission?

> **Time-Out #4**
> Pass around a hand-held mirror to everyone in the class. Have each person hold the mirror, look at his/her reflection, and think of one way he/she can improve spiritually before passing it on to the next person.

Taking It Home

Pick out one of the practices from Time-Out #3 that you think will help you spend more time in God's Word. Try it out this week, and see if you can make it a habit!

Chapter 4

Playing Favorites
James 2:1-13

James begins this chapter with an illustration. Let's update it and see how it sounds: Your family is hosting a youth group devotional one Sunday night, and your living room is packed with people. Just as you are about to start singing the first song, the door opens, and two individuals enter the house. You recognize the first one immediately – Kristin Johnson! You knew some of the girls in the youth group had invited her, but you can't believe she actually came to your house! She is not only one of the most popular girls in school, but she is definitely the best looking cheerleader in your grade. Her father owns a printing company, and the new house they built last year was the talk of the school. It was constructed like a celebrity's mansion, complete with an in-ground pool outside and a theater room inside! Your sister, who is a year younger than you, complains that Kristin and her friends are mean to the other girls at school, sitting at their lunch table and making fun of anyone they don't think is cool enough. You forget about all that when Kristin's eyes meet yours and she asks, "Where should I sit?" You almost trip over yourself taking her coat and pointing to the overstuffed recliner by the television; one of your friends made the mistake of getting up for a minute, so Kristin gets the best seat in the house! Once she sits down, you glance over and see who came in behind her.

Ron is a nice enough guy, but you find yourself wondering who invited him to this devo. He sits in front of you in Algebra, and he keeps to himself most of the time. Everyone knew about the layoffs at the plant, and you had heard that Ron's dad lost his job. They had to move out of their house and into a cheap apartment downtown. Ron's hair seems to be constantly messed up, and he is wearing a blue jean jacket that looks like it was bought at Goodwill and has clearly seen better days. You almost forget about the time you were lost in Algebra and Ron took a few minutes after school to explain the last three chapters to you before your mid-tern exam. That all comes flooding back when Ron says, "Hey! I haven't talked to you much since our big study session. Where should I sit?" You can feel the eyes of everyone, including Kristin, focused on you and your reaction. You look around frantically and grab an old couch cushion from the playroom and toss it in the back doorway, practically in the hall. Ron gives you a half-smile, then settles into his spot at the back of the group while you walk over to your seat, which just happens to be next to Kristin's. She nods at Ron, rolls her eyes, and smiles at you. You smile back, feeling simultaneously sorry for Ron but thrilled at sharing an inside joke with the most popular girl in school!

Who Are Your True Friends?

The situation James describes is similar the one above. In James' time, the Romans maintained a strict class system. Your wealth, family history, and occupation determined your class. Upper class individuals dressed like the rich man in James' story – sporting gold jewelry and clothes that were "fine," usually shiny and bright to show they were expensive. The poor man in James' story clearly has neither. Associating with people who were in classes below yours was heavily discouraged. If Christians weren't careful, the same class system could exist in their congregations, prizing the rich, powerful convert over the poor, dirty man who became a Christian. James' message is clear – there are no second-class citizens of the kingdom of God; every Christian should be welcomed, loved, and treated equally.

Time-Out #1

The book of James, as well as the rest of the Bible, is just as relevant today as it was then. You have seen people excluded or made fun of because of their social status, haven't you? If we're honest, we can probably admit that we have avoided others for that same reason. Take a minute to think of someone you have excluded before simply because he wasn't popular or she didn't wear the right clothes. Write his or her name down. No one else has to see this; it is between you and God. Then, pray for that person. Hold on to that post-it and put in your wallet or inside your locker. Pray for that person every day for a week, and see what happens!

Rich or Poor?

God chose the poor of this world to be rich in faith, according to verse 5, and Jesus' life is evidence of that fact. Think about how Jesus came into the world. God could have chosen any way He wanted to have His Son come live among the people He created. Jesus could have been born into a wealthy home, or He could have been the son of a well-known Pharisee. Instead, He was the son of a working class carpenter (Mark 6:3). Jesus could have been born in a palace, but His birth took place in a smelly manger (ok, so Luke 2:7 doesn't exactly state that the manger smelled, but have you ever been inside a barn before?). Jesus could have come to Earth as the best-looking guy around, drawing people to Him simply because of His appearance. While we know Jesus had a loving spirit that drew people to Him, Isaiah prophesied in Isaiah 53:2 that Jesus would have "no beauty or majesty to attract us to Him, nothing in His appearance that we should desire Him." In other words, Jesus was not from a rich family, didn't live in the best neighbor-

Time-Out #2

Break the class up into two groups. Have Group #1 brainstorm the ingredients for being popular – what is it that makes someone popular at school? Then, have that same group brainstorm the ingredients for being unpopular. Have Group #2 brainstorm Scriptures in which God describes how He wants Christians to act, as well as passages that show actions God wants us to avoid. After a few minutes, have both groups compare lists. What are the differences in what the world wants on a person and what God wants? What are the differences in what the world dislikes and what God dislikes? Are there any items the world values that God doesn't? What about vice-versa?

hood, and wasn't the best looking guy in town. If someone like that attended your school, would he be popular or unpopular?

You're From Where?

Verse 4 reminds us that when we make those distinctions, we become judges with evil motives. After all, our motive is selfish in excluding certain people and accepting others. We do it so that the "important" people at school or work will like us more. Have you ever noticed that the popular people who we want to impress so badly are often the people that make our life miserable when we do something embarrassing? The same principle held true in James' day. The rich people were the ones oppressing Christians. Many Christians would have been poor, and they were apparently dragged into court by wealthier landowners, who would cheat them out of what little money they had (James has more to say about the way rich people are misusing their wealth in chapter 5). Why would they want to impress people who were oppressing them? Why do we want people to like us who would just as soon make fun of us?

Many times, we can be "judges with evil motives" without even realizing it. We are often tempted to make snap judgments based strictly on appearances. Jesus dealt with those same challenges. Nathanael first heard about Jesus when Philip told him that Jesus was from Nazareth (not exactly the most influential town). Nathanael responded by asking, "Can anything good come out of Nazareth?" (John 1:46). He eventually got past his impression of Jesus' hometown. When Jesus preached to the crowds in the synagogue, He boldly told them His mission as the Son of God. They responded by saying, "Isn't this the carpenter's son? Isn't his mother's name Mary, and aren't his brothers James, Joseph, Simon, and Judas? Aren't all his sisters with us? Where then did this man get all these things?" (Matthew 13:55-56). They couldn't look past the child they had watched grow and see the Son of God that had come to save their sins. Here was God in the flesh, and they were missing the point because of these outward impressions. Jesus, on the other hand, looked past appearances and into hearts.

Time-Out #3

Throughout His ministry, Jesus spent time with those who were poor, hurting, and excluded. As a class, brainstorm all the situations you can think of in which Jesus reached out to those who were left out of the "in crowd."

That's Not a Big Deal...Right?

Toward the end of this passage, James tackles a thought that was as common then as it is today, the idea that some sins are big and others are little. We usually think of "big" sins, like murder, rape, or adultery as being much worse than "little" sins like lying, cheating, or gossiping. Of course, some sins have greater consequences than others, but all sin breaks the heart of our God. James states in verse 9 that showing favoritism is a sin – and even if we haven't committed one of the "big ones," when we show favoritism we are just as guilty of sin as someone who has. He also references the second "greatest command" in verse 8 and reminds us that showing favoritism breaks what Jesus said was at the heart of discipleship: loving your neighbor. No matter what our friends at school think is cool or funny, favoritism is neither. It is serious business.

Time-Out #4

As a class, list some of the sins we usually view as "big sins." Now, list the sins we usually think of "little sins." Why do you think we make that distinction? What are some lasting results of the "little sins?" Have each person choose one of the "little sins" that is the most difficult to resist. Then, take a few minutes of silent prayer time for each individual to bring that sin before God and ask for His strength in dealing with the temptation.

Verse 12 and 13 show us the end result of this teaching. We need to live as people who have been shown mercy, judged by a law that gives freedom. If we choose not to live that way, and show no mercy, then we can't expect our God to show mercy to us. The same principle Jesus mentioned when He talked about judging in Matthew 7:2 is present here – the way we judge others on earth affects the way we are going to be judged. If God has shown us incredible mercy, why wouldn't we show that same mercy to everyone else? For James, the choice was easy – show mercy and uphold God's law. Let's make the same decision.

Putting It All Together

1. Imagine the cafeteria at your school. Picture the different tables where everyone sits. Think of the groups at each one. If Jesus were attending your school, where would He sit during lunch? Now, for a tougher question…would you be willing to sit at His table, even if it meant sitting by outcasts?

2. Who does James say are "rich in faith" and "heirs of the kingdom"?

3. Verse 7 tells us that showing favoritism shows blasphemy against God's name. Blasphemy is the sin of saying something about God that isn't

true. The Jews often accused Jesus of blasphemy when He claimed to be the Son of God. As Christians, when we show favoritism, we are saying something about God that isn't true. What message does favoritism communicate?

4.   Does this mean you can't have friends that you spend more time with than others? Why or why not?

5.   What does "mercy" mean? How can you show it to others?

Taking It Home

Think about that person whose name you wrote down. In addition to praying for that person, what is one thing you can do this week to make that person's day better? It could be as simple as inviting him to eat lunch with you or even talking to her in the hallway before school. Pray for that person, and then let God use you to be part of the answer to that prayer!

Chapter 5

Your Faith—Dead or Alive?
James 2:14-26

February 16th, 2007 started as just an ordinary day for the Suffolk County Police in Hampton Bays, New York. Nothing too exciting was on tap, until a routine investigation of bursted water pipes in a house revealed a shocking secret. Vincenzo Ricardo, the 70-year-old owner of the house, was dead in his chair. His neighbors had been the ones who reported the bursted pipes, and as the police entered the home, they found Vincenzo's body still in his chair, with the T.V. still blaring. It was determined by the chief medical examiner that he died of natural causes. Although unusual, it still sounds fairly routine doesn't it? It does, until one small detail is included: Vincenzo had been dead for an entire year!

Ricardo lived with his wife, until her passing a few years earlier. After that, he lived alone and kept to himself. None of the neighbors had thought about checking on him; many assumed that he had been moved to a nursing home or long-term healthcare facility. The police weren't sure how his power was still on and how no one noticed his death. They also weren't sure how long it would have taken to discover him had the water pipes not burst.

This story caught the nation's attention, because no one could imagine someone being dead for so long without anyone knowing. In the latter half of James 2, James refers to another death whose consequences are even more serious than the death of a physical body – the death of faith. He states in verse 17 that faith without works is dead, and we know that a dead faith won't save us. It is scary to think of someone being dead without anyone else knowing, but it is even scarier to think of our faith being dead without anyone noticing. That's why James' examination of faith in these verses is incredibly important. He tells us exactly what we need in order to have saving faith, and he warns us about the danger of dead faith. By paying attention to his words, we won't have to worry about anyone discovering dead faith in our lives.

Faith OR Works? It is Not a Choice.

We all have faith in something. When we board a plane, we have faith that the pilot is trained and capable of flying an aircraft. When we sit in a dentist's chair, we have faith that the dentist actually attended dental school and knows how to take care of teeth. Not only do we have faith in these situations, but that faith changes the way we act. If a pilot tells us to buckle our seatbelts, we do it. If a dentist tells us not to eat for thirty minutes after a visit, we follow those instructions. Can you imagine telling a pilot that you trust him, but you don't want to get on the plane? Is that trust? What about saying to a dentist that you have faith in her wisdom, but you have decided to completely disregard her instructions to brush your teeth daily? Is that faith? If we didn't follow it up with action, our faith wouldn't be worth much, would it?

Time-Out #1

Ask for one or two volunteers to illustrate faith by doing a "trust fall." Ask them to stand up straight, and then fall backward into the waiting arms of a few classmates. How does it feel to put your trust into someone else? What if you told your friends you trusted them to catch you, yet you refused to fall backward? Do you think they would believe you?

James makes it abundantly clear that faith does not exist without works, or action. Usually, we think of faith as the inward belief in something and works as the deeds we do that everyone can see. James is saying that what we do on the outside proves what we believe on the inside. Both are necessary; we can't choose one over the other. To prove this, he uses a vivid example. Imagine a Christian who needs food. If someone tells that hungry Christian, "I hope you feel better. I know you are hungry and I want you to get something to eat," and yet he doesn't feed that person, what is the use? If he really wanted to help, wouldn't he have fed the starving individual? In verse 17, James states that telling a person to be fed without feeding them is like saying you have faith without having any works. It isn't possible.

Time-Out #2

Work through Hebrews 11 as a class, and find the repeating pattern in each character description. Make a list on the board of each name and then what he or she did to prove faithful. After you have made the list, have each student write down his/her name and take a moment to think of what he/she could do to prove faithful to God.

Hebrews 11 helps us understand faith's core definition. In verse 1, faith is described as being "sure of what we hope for and certain of what we do not see." Verse 2 reminds us that the ancient followers of God were commended for their faith, and verse 6 tells us that without faith, we cannot please God. This sets the tone for a chapter full of faithful examples. Noah, Moses – there are all kinds of individuals listed who faithfully served God. As you read through the chapter, you will notice a pattern. By faith, each individual *did something*. By faith, Noah built an ark. By faith, Moses left Egypt. Each individual not only believed in God, but did something to prove that belief. Faith cannot exist without works.

Faith *vs.* Works? It is Not a War.

Sometimes we are tempted to think that belief alone is enough. In other words, as long as I believe in God, I don't need any works – just belief. In fact, there are even religious organizations with the slogan "Only Believe." Did you notice the way James approaches this idea? He reminds us in verse 19 that even demons believe in God, and shudder! For an example, check out Mark 5:1-13, when Jesus cast the demons out of the man in the Gerasenes. Even before Jesus got close, the demons knew Him and were upset that He had arrived. They begged Him to go into the pigs, and they did only after Jesus gave them permission. Other passages, such as Luke 4:41, reinforce the fact that demons recognized Jesus and He had power over them. James refers to these instances by saying, "You believe in Jesus? Good – the demons He cast out believe in Him too."

Paul had a lot to say about faith and works, and when his writings are compared with this passage, it seems confusing. For instance, in Romans 4:1-5, Paul uses Abraham as an example of someone who is saved by faith in God. In James 3:20-24, James uses Abraham as an example of someone whose works prove his faith. They both quote from Genesis 15:6, which states that Abraham believed in God and it was credited to him as righteousness. Are they contradicting each other? Did Paul preach faith while James preferred works? How do these two passages fit together?

Whenever we read Scripture, it is important to understand the context – what has been written earlier, the purpose of the letter, the identity of the original audience, etc. In Romans, Paul is writing to both Jewish and Gentile Christians who are battling over outward signs of the Old Law, like circumcision. James is writing to Jewish Christians who have been scattered out through Judea and Samaria. He and Paul are dealing with two different extremes: Paul is correcting Christians who are so concerned with outward signs that they have lost sight of faith's true meaning, and James is dealing with Christians who are living around non-Christians and have lost sight of how to show their faith. Imagine that you are driving down a two lane mountain road. If you veer into the left lane, you are headed straight for the opposite lane of traffic. If you drift to the right, you will sail off the side of the mountain and onto the rocks below. Both options would mean serious injury, maybe even death. Paul and James are writing to readers in danger of veering off the road in two separate directions, and these inspired writers want both groups to come back to the middle ground: an accurate understanding of faith and works.

When James describes Abraham's faith, he provides a clue to help us understand the relationship between faith and works. He writes in verse 22 that Abraham's faith was made complete by what he did. Yes, Abraham was righteous because of his faith, but that faith was made possible only by his works. Even Rahab, someone whose previous life was definitely not full of righteous works, was viewed as righteous because she believed the Israelite spies and took care of them (Joshua 6:25). Her faith needed works to be complete. When we read through the New Testament, we find out that obedient faith includes confessing our belief in Jesus, repenting of our sins and turning our lives around, being baptized, and living a life dedicated to serving God. Our faith is not complete, until we prove it with our works, and these actions are what God has designed to place us into His family. This is not a war, in which we have to choose either a life of faith or a life of works. They belong together, because neither one is complete without the other.

Faith *AND* Works – It is a Way of Life

If works don't earn our salvation, then why are they important to complete our faith? Paul sheds some light on this in Ephesians 2:8-10, in which he tells us that we aren't saved by works, but we are created to do good works. When we do good works, we are fulfilling the purpose God has set out for us. He would also write in Romans 8:12 about the debt we owe to Christ. It makes sense; once we realize what God has done for us, we should want to serve Him. Not that we could ever pay Him back, but that we should show how much we appreciate His grace. How many times have we heard about a soldier who dove on a grenade to save the lives of those who fought alongside him, or a policeman who sacrificed his life for an innocent bystander? In those cases, the people who were saved have an entirely new perspective on life. They often live the rest of their lives in an attempt to honor the one who saved them. They can't ever fully repay that individual, but they respond in gratitude with their works. The better we understand the Christ's sacrifice, the more we will desire to serve Him.

Time-Out #3

In Ephesians 2:10, Paul tells us there are some good works Jesus has prepared in advance. That means there are some good works that God wants every one of us to accomplish. Divide into groups, and have each person share a "good work" that teens can do in your congregation. Then, have each person share a "good work" he or she can do to represent Christ at school.

One More Word About Works

Imagine that you have received a birthday present from your best friend. She spent a lot of money on you, and it is the perfect gift – one you had your eye on for months. Take a second to imagine what that gift would be. She hands it to you, all wrapped up in beautiful paper with a huge ribbon. Now, if you leave it in the wrapping paper, that gift won't be worth much to you, will it? In order to enjoy the gift, you have to unwrap it. But we all know that by taking off the wrapping paper, you didn't earn that gift. Your friend saved up her money and spent it on you. You are getting it for free, but you won't be able to enjoy it unless you do something to access it.

That illustration has been used often over the years, and it helps us understand the purpose of works. Our works don't earn us the gift of salvation, but the only way we can access this incredible gift is by taking action. When we act on our faith, putting Christ on in baptism, and continue to remain faithful, living for Him, we access the greatest gift ever. We don't gain salvation by works, but we can't access it without them. It is not enough to talk the talk of faith; we must also walk the walk by our works.

Putting It All Together

1.   What is a definition of "faith"?

2.   Can you think of an Old Testament hero who wasn't included in Hebrews 11 but displayed faith in action?

3.   What about some New Testament Christians who did the same thing?

4.   How would you describe the relationship between faith and works?

5.   If someone said you didn't need to repent or be baptized because those were just "works," how would you respond?

Taking It Home

During this week's lesson, your class talked a lot about faith. Take a few minutes during this week to think of faithful individuals who have made a difference in your life. Make your own personal "Hebrews 11 Heroes of Faith List." You might even want to write a note to those people and let them know what they mean to you.

Time-Out #4

Close by writing "FAITH" on the board and asking the class to list everything that faith includes. Afterward, let each student know that you are available if anyone has questions about becoming a Christian or is interested in further Bible study.

Chapter 6

Taming the Tongue
James 3:1-12

Let's say you were preparing to go to battle, and you needed a powerful weapon that was capable of destroying several enemy buildings and taking out miles of enemy territory. Would you be thinking of missiles, bombs, or maybe a new military vehicle with all the bells and whistles? Can you imagine the shock if you were handed a match? One single match isn't a very powerful weapon...is it?

In October of 2007, dry and windy conditions caused several wildfires to rage for days in California. One of the blazes, called the "Buckweed Fire" burned almost sixty square miles and totally destroyed 21 houses in Los Angeles County. Many of these wildfires are begun by arsonists, and inspectors investigated carefully for signs of foul play. What they found was a young boy, under the age of 13, who admitted to playing with matches and accidentally starting a fire. A fire that raged for days began with a match that flamed for seconds. We might not realize it, but a match can be a deadly weapon.

Why Bother?

One of the images James uses to describe the power of the tongue is a spark, or small flame (3:5). It may be small, but it packs a big punch. James tells us that if we don't do our best to control it, we are playing with fire. Obviously, none of us is perfect, and everybody will struggle with saying things they shouldn't say. James even says so in verse 2, writing that every person struggles in many ways, and only a perfect man can avoid making mistakes in what he says. He also admits in verse 8 that no man can tame the tongue. If that is true, why try?

We would never dream of handing a gun to a soldier without training him in how to use it, and letting someone go hunting with a loaded crossbow and no experience shooting one would not be smart. Yet, every one of us possesses a tongue that is capable of doing serious damage, and we need to train ourselves how to use it properly. The New Testament is clear that none of us is perfect (Romans 3:23; 1 John 1:10), but that doesn't mean we stop trying to serve God or allow ourselves to sin more. It means that we realize our limitations as we do our absolute best to follow God's will. The same principle is true for dealing with our words. Read verses 1-12 to see some truths necessary for "tongue-taming."

Time-Out #1

Ask for a volunteer who doesn't mind trying something new! Blindfold that individual and give them plastic gloves to wear (trust me, they will come in handy!). Now watch this gullible...I mean...willing volunteer try to identify several objects by holding them. What do they all have in common?

Truth #1—Teach the Right Message

James begins this chapter by saying not many of his readers should become teachers (vs. 1). That seems like a strange way for a New Testament writer to talk to Christians, not to mention a challenge for anyone who is trying to recruit teachers for a Bible class! Shouldn't we all want to be teachers? He also states that teachers will receive stricter judgment. There's another strange statement. Is James saying that teachers are held to a different standard than other Christians?

Here are a couple of things to remember as we read this passage. *First of all, teachers face serious temptations.* In James' time, not everyone in a congregation could read. Because of the class system in place, it would have been difficult for those in the lower social classes to receive education. Those who could read and teach others were held in high regard; they had a powerful position. That kind of power can go to a person's head. Early Christians struggled with pride just like we do. In 3 John 1:9, the apostle John writes about a man named Diotrephes who loved to "be first among them." Because of his love of the limelight, he was resisting the teaching of John. Paul dealt with a similar problem in 1 Corinthians. The Corinthian Christians were dividing up according to which teacher they liked the best. 1 Corinthians 1:12 tells us that some were claiming to follow the teaching of Paul, some Apollos, some Peter, and some Christ (as if Paul, Apollos, and Peter weren't encouraging the Corinthian Christians to follow Christ). Teachers have to be careful not to fall into the trap of pride.

Secondly, teachers have a serious responsibility. When we are sharing God's Word, we need to be certain that what we are teaching is true. Have you ever stopped to think about some of the harshest words Jesus used during His ministry? They were usually directed at the Pharisees. In Matthew 23, we read the "Eight Woes" spoken to the Pharisees. Jesus called them "blind guides" (vs. 16) and said that through their teaching they were shutting off the Kingdom of Heaven from people (vs. 13). They were supposed to be the teachers of the Law, but because they were teaching inaccurately, they were discouraging others from following Christ. When James says that not many should be teachers, he is reminding all of us that teaching carries with it an obligation that

Time-Out #2

We like to talk…probably too much. One estimate recently reported that if we took the average amount of words an individual speaks in one day and typed them all out on paper, we would have 52 sheets of paper filled with words. Can you imagine a stack of pages to hold all the words you said in a week? What about a month? How many of those words would be positive, and how many would you wish you could take back?

none of us can take lightly. This principle doesn't apply only to Bible class teachers, either. Every single Christian is a teacher, because we have the opportunity to share God's Word with others every day. Whether it is talking to a friend on

Time-Out #3

Try this exercise: have everyone in the room remain in complete silence for an entire minute. No talking, no movement, just silence. A minute doesn't seem like a long time when we are talking, but staying quiet for that long reminds us of how we avoid silence.

the way home from school or studying the Bible with a visitor on a youth retreat, we each have the responsibility to share God's truth accurately.

Truth #2—Talk the Right Talk

As you can see, we talk a lot. We don't usually leave much time in our schedules for silence. As soon as we get in the car, we turn on the radio. As soon as we get home, we turn on the television. We might sing, "Be still and know that I am God," in devotionals, but it is hard for us to put that into practice.

Negative words can leave a lasting imprint. Did you notice something all the images in the first few verses of James 3 have in common? A horse, a ship, a fire: all are powerful images. The tongue is powerful, and that power is not always used for good. Whoever came up with the phrase, "Sticks and stones may break my bones, but words will never hurt me," might have found a catchy slogan, but it isn't a true one. The pain of negative words can last longer than a physical injury, and the bruises left are just as real.

Positive words can make an impact as well. Proverbs 25:11 states that words "fitly spoken" are like apples of gold in settings of silver. In other words, positive words spoken at just the right time are priceless. We know that is true, because each of us has experienced it. Think back to those stacks of paper. When we think about the negative potential our words have, those stacks might seem like powerful ways to hurt others. But if we focus on the positive ways our words can lift someone up, the stacks become incredible opportunities to build up those around us.

If you ever wonder whether or not you should say something, ask yourself a few questions. Turn to Ephesians 4, where Paul gives us instruction on how to speak – 1. Is it true? (vs. 25), 2. Is it wholesome? (vs. 29), 3. Does it build someone up? (vs. 29) 4. Is it bitter or angry? (vs. 31), 5. Is it kind? (vs. 32) This list is not exhaustive, but it is helpful. If we stop and think about what we say, we are less likely to let some negative words slip. Have you ever written something in an IM or e-mail and then stopped to re-read your own words? It is so easy to send off an e-mail quickly and regret it as soon as we press "send." Let's take our time and think about our words.

> **Time-Out #4**
> Stop for a minute and think about a time someone gave you just the encouragement or compliment you needed. Share it with the class. How did it make you feel?

Truth #3—Walk the Right Walk

James goes on to tell us that it isn't enough just to talk like a Christian; we have to live like it. There are several ways in which we can use our words in ways that aren't Christ-like, but we will focus on a couple of common temptations.

1. Lying: In the grand scheme of things, lying doesn't seem like too big a sin, does it? We live in a world where shootings, abuse, and other violent crimes are constantly reported on television and the internet. With that in mind, lying can seem pretty insignificant. If your parents ask where you are going when you take off with your friends on Friday night, is it really that big a deal if you don't tell them exactly where you will be? When your teacher asks if the work you are turning in is your own, is it that big a deal if you say yes when the answer is no?

Scripture makes the answers to all these questions clear – yes. In fact, when the Old Testament records a list of sins that God hates, lying makes the cut. Proverbs 6:16-19 lists seven things that God hates, and lying is on the list…twice! Verse 17 mentions a lying tongue, while verse 19 includes a false witness who spreads lies. The first reference reminds us that any lie is a sin, while the second one seems to refer to a person who would provide false testimony in order to convict an innocent person. Before we decide lying isn't that big a deal, we need to realize that God hates it. Our Creator *hates* lying.

Not only that, but when we lie, we are not speaking God's language. Jesus gives us insight into this principle in John 8:44, when He tells the Jews that Satan is the father of all lies. According to Jesus, when Satan lies, he speaks his natural language. The next time you are tempted to tell a lie, no matter how insignificant it may seem, remind yourself that if you do, you will be speaking the language of Satan. The flip side of that principle is seen throughout the Bible as God's Words are always held up as truth. Given the choice, whose language would we rather speak?

Sometimes we are tempted to tell half-truths, to mislead someone without actually lying. For instance, when your parents ask who is going to be at your friends' house, you might not tell them all the names (especially if they are names of friends your parents don't want you to hang around). That's not really a lie, is it? Maybe an Old Testament story can help us out here. Abraham used the same half-truth twice, in Genesis 12 on Pharaoh and Genesis 20 on King Abimelech. Both times Abraham tells these powerful men that his wife Sarah is his sister. Technically, because of the family situation, she was his half-sister (20:12). But both times, God intervened, sending a plague on Pharaoh's house and giving a chilling message to Abimelech. Abraham didn't tell the whole truth, and there were consequences. We need to be careful not to make the same mistake.

2. Cursing: I know what you're thinking – the word "cursing" usually brings to mind a list of a few words we shouldn't say. The biblical definition of cursing, though, includes that but also extends far beyond it. In verse 9, James talks about the human temptation to bless God one minute, then turn around and curse others the next. He reminds us that all men are made in the image of God. The next time you are tempted to insult that guy in your science class or talk about that girl who always makes fun of you behind her back, remember that they are individuals made in the image of God. Do we really have the right to verbally hurt individuals who are made in His image?

It's not just our words that are the problem; it is the motivation behind them. Jesus made it clear that what we say comes from what we have in our heart (Matthew 12:34). In the Sermon on the Mount, Jesus addresses that issue when He talks about murder (Matthew 5:21, 22). He stresses that murder is bad, but so is calling someone a fool. Harshly insulting others usually reflects an ungodly feeling in our hearts, and that same feeling is what often leads to murder. Just because we don't commit murder doesn't mean it is okay to hold that hatred in our hearts and insult others.

Another aspect of cursing that God is clear about in Scripture is taking His name in vain. Jewish scribes had an interesting practice when it came to saying God's name. While there is more than one way to say God in Hebrew, the name which we know as Yaweh (or Jehovah) was usually considered the "holy" name for God. We aren't even sure exactly how to pronounce it, because they were so reluctant to say it. When it came time to write it down, they would stop to bathe themselves, change clothes, write it down, and then repeat the process. That might sound extreme to us, but it was an effective way to insure that no one took the name of God lightly. As Christians, we are called to honor the same God they served by the way we use our tongues.

Putting It All Together
1. Why does James say we should be careful about becoming teachers?
2. Why is controlling the tongue so important? Why is it such a challenge?
3. How does James describe the tongue?
4. Can you think of common lies we are tempted to tell?
5. Can you think of some ways we are tempted to take God's name in vain?

Taking It Home
Think of someone you can share some positive encouragement with this week, and do it. You might be surprised at the difference it makes!

Chapter 7

Wise Up
James 3:13-18

A famous story told about an old philosopher will help us understand the importance James places on wisdom. Socrates, an ancient teacher, once had a young student walk up to him. He asked Socrates how to gain wisdom. Socrates said nothing and began walking. The young man followed him, until they reached a river. Socrates then began to wade into the water. The young student followed, and once they were both in the water, Socrates asked him, "What do you want?" The man said, "Wisdom." Socrates promptly grabbed the young man and shoved his head under the water. He held him there for 30 seconds, and then raised him out of the water. "What do you want?" he asked again. Again, the young man said, "Wisdom." Socrates did the same thing, this time holding him under for 40 seconds. When he asked the question a third time, the student again answered, "Wisdom." Socrates proceeded to hold his head under for 50 seconds. The young man's lungs burned, and he feared he would drown. When Socrates asked again, "What do you want?" the young man said, "I want to breathe!" Socrates then answered, "When you want wisdom as badly as you wanted air, then you will find it." How badly do we want wisdom? James teaches us that we should eagerly desire godly wisdom, and he tells us exactly how to get it.

It Seemed Like a Good Idea...

If you think about it, you can probably remember making a decision that seemed good at the time but turned out to be unwise. In fact, even major companies have made that mistake. In the late 1950's, the Ford Motor Company made what seemed like a great choice at the time. They sunk thousands of dollars and years of research into developing an experimental car, or "E-car." It was going to feature all the latest innovations, and part of its premiere included a top-rated T.V. show. The name of the car was the Ford Edsel, and it sounded like a good idea. Less than four years after its debut, the Edsel was discontinued. It went down as one of the worst ideas in automobile history.

Only a few decades later, another major company needed a shot in the arm. Coca-Cola® was losing ground to Pepsi®, a soft drink that was becoming increasingly popular. They took a bold step, reformulating the time-tested Coca-Cola recipe and coming out with a completely new drink. They introduced "New Coke" on April 23, 1985. While it appeared to be a success at first, the company returned to the old formula within three months. A vocal opposition and failing sales forced them to realize their mistake. It is known as one of the most infamous flops in business history.

While these famous mistakes are entertaining to read about, they weren't all that fun for those companies to experience. In the same way, it doesn't feel good to play our mental "highlight reel" of all the mistakes we've made in the past. The rules we have broken, the times we've mistreated our friends – they may have even seemed like good ideas at the time. There is a kind of wisdom we see all around us, a worldly wisdom, that promotes those ideas. It is the kind of wisdom that tells us cheating is the smart thing to do, as long as we don't get caught. It tells us that lies are okay, if they get us out of trouble. In this passage, James teaches us how to spot that earthly wisdom and instead use godly wisdom to make good decisions. Will we live perfect lives? No. There has only been one perfect Man to walk this earth, but understanding James's teaching will prepare us to make better decisions.

Why Do We Need Wisdom?

We know wisdom is incredibly important, because God says so over and over in the Bible. One of the books of poetry in the Old Testament, Proverbs, is filled with reminders of why wisdom matters. Proverbs 4:5 tells us, "Get wisdom, get understanding; do not forget my words or swerve from them." Verse 7 goes on to say, "Wisdom is supreme; therefore get wisdom. Though it cost you all you have, get understanding." Can you feel the urgency behind that statement? Wisdom is worth everything you have.

In the Old Testament, two kings show us that principle in action. When Solomon first became king, God came to him and told him to ask for whatever he wanted. Solomon did exactly what the Proverbs say – he asked for wisdom (1 Kings 3:5-9). When his son, Rehoboam, came to power, he was faced with a choice. He was asked by the people if he would be as hard on them as his father was. He got advice from two groups: the older advisors who had served his father, and the younger advisors who had grown up with him. Rather than choose the wisdom of the older advisors, he stuck with what his friends told him (1 Kings 12:8). As a result, the kingdom eventually split. Two young rulers: one understood the importance of wisdom, and one didn't.

How Can We Recognize Worldly Wisdom?

James gives us a clear description of what godly wisdom is not. Notice the phrases and concepts he uses – bitter jealousy, selfish ambition, boasting, untruth, and disorder, just to name a few. All these are markers of worldly or "unspiritual" wisdom. In verse 15, James tells us that this kind of wisdom is demonic. Some versions translate the term "devilish," and it literally means "from the devil." Take a minute to think about that – when you use the wisdom of the world, you are taking a cue from Satan, thinking exactly the way he wants you to think.

Time-Out #1

What would you do if God offered you anything you wanted? Make a list on the board of all the possibilities – what sounds the best to you? Once you have something in mind, ask yourself if you would trade that for wisdom. What does that tell you about wisdom's importance?

We don't have to look far in the Bible to find people using this type of logic. After delivering Noah and his family from the flood, God specifically told him and his family to fill the earth (Genesis 9:1). It is only a few chapters later, however, when we find a group of people leaving God's commands behind to follow worldly wisdom. In Genesis 11:4, they decide they want to build a city, make a name for themselves, and build a tower so they wouldn't be scattered over the earth.

Jesus tells a parable about someone with a similar mindset in Luke 12:13-21. When he brought all his crops in, he realized that he didn't have nearly enough room in his old barns, and he decided to tear those down and build all new barns. He doesn't seem concerned about helping anyone else or sharing with those who might need it; he is only thinking about himself. Jesus ends that parable by saying that the man's soul would be demanded from him. Talk about a shocking ending – can you imagine how Jesus' audience would reacted when the main character in his story died at the end?

How Do We Know God's Wisdom?

Now that we have wrapped our minds around worldly wisdom, let's focus on God's wisdom. James uses a completely different set of words to talk about this kind of wisdom: pure, peace-loving, considerate, submissive, full of mercy and good fruit, impartial, and sincere (vss. 17, 18). Did you notice the difference? Think of a person who usually gives you good advice. Chances are, that person's wisdom sounds more like this description than the previous one.

We see individuals who display godly wisdom in Scripture as well. For an example, let's think about James himself. You know how frustrating it is when someone tells you to act a certain way, but he doesn't live that way himself? That is not what James is doing; we know from Scripture that he lived the lessons he taught. For example, in Acts 15, we read about a big meeting of elders in the church and apostles about an important issue. Some teachers were saying that Gentiles (people who weren't Jews) had to live by the Jewish Old Testament laws like circumcision. We know from other New Testament writings that we live under the New Covenant, but this was a difficult transition for many of the people living in the first century, so church leaders gathered in Jerusalem to discuss it.

Just imagine how tense that would be, a huge crowd of people who are upset and debating with each other. Verse 7 tells us that the discussion lasted a long time,

Time-Out #2

Let's stop for a second and think about those two passages. Pick one volunteer to stand in front of the class and say loudly, "Let's build a city, make a name for ourselves, and build a tower." (If the volunteer wants to use a crazy voice, that is always a plus!) Now, stop and go through the worldly wisdom checklist — bitter envy, selfish ambition, boasting, untruth, and disorder. Which of these elements can you hear in that statement from the Tower of Babel? Now, choose another volunteer to say this, "This is what I'll do; I'll tear down my barns and build bigger ones. Then, I'll say to myself, 'You have plenty of good things stored up for many years. Take life easy — eat, drink, and be merry.'" (Again, it is important that the volunteer has a lot of fun with it.) Take another look at the checklist and find out which phrases describe that statement.

Time-Out #3

Read through the following examples, and see which ones pass the James 3 wisdom test. Decide which wisdom is from the world and which is from God. Try to name the specific elements found in each one.

1. "It's only a homework assignment, so you can just copy my answers. Besides, it's not like she ever checks our work. You might as well go for a good grade – that's what matters."

2. "It serves him right; he should know that if he acts that way, people are going to make fun of him. I know I wouldn't want to be seen with him."

3. "I know she's your friend, but you really shouldn't lie to your parents just to go to a party. Even if they never find out, it still isn't right."

4. "He is always getting all the attention on youth group trips, just because he is so nice to everyone and he always gets asked to speak on retreats. If you know something embarrassing about him and you want to tell everybody, I say go for it. It will be hilarious, and maybe you can get some of that attention."

5. "You may be right, but think of her feelings. This could really hurt her. I would pray about it before you talk with her."

and then Peter stepped up and made a statement. After him, Paul and Barnabas began to speak. When they were done, James stood up and showed God's wisdom. He mentioned what Peter had said, and then he quoted Scripture. After that, he stated in verse 19 that in his judgment they shouldn't make things more difficult for Gentiles by making the keep the Law of Moses. Did you catch the wisdom there? He looked at what was being said, compared it to Scripture, and made a judgment. He was peaceful in a time when debate was raging. He was considerate during an argument, and he made an impartial decision. In verse 28, we read that the Holy Spirit was present, guiding this decision. When we use godly wisdom, God will help us make good choices.

How Do We Show Wisdom?

Now that we know how to identify true wisdom from Satan's counterfeit version, the next step is focusing on how we can be wiser in our daily lives. In his book, James gives us three specific ways we can grow in wisdom every day. In 3:13, he tells us that wise deeds are done in humility or "meekness." In 3:18, we find out that truly wise people are peace-makers who "sow peace." And, you might remember that way back in 1:5, James told his readers to pray for wisdom and they would receive it. Those are three major ways we can improve in the wisdom department.

1. Live Meekly. The word "meekness" sounds so much like "weakness," we usually don't think of a meek person as being strong. In fact, we might think of a meek person as someone who can't defend himself or doesn't speak up for herself. Actually, nothing could be further from the truth. The ancient Greeks had a word picture they used to describe meekness, and it is a great way for us to understand it. The definition of meekness is power under control, and the Greeks would compare it to a wild horse that had been broken. A wild horse has great power, but no one can control it. Once a horse is broken, a rider can place a saddle on it, put a bit in its mouth, and control it with reins. The horse is not suddenly weaker, just submissive. That is the picture of meekness – having power under control.

Jesus was a meek man. We sometimes sing phrases like, "And yet no friend is so meek and lowly," without stopping to think about what that means. Imagine that you had the power of Jesus as you walked around from day to day. Anytime someone insulted you, made fun of you, or annoyed you, you could snap your fingers and perform a miracle. Wouldn't it be tempting to do that? Jesus was constantly confronted by people who were challenging Him, but He never used His power to show off. He would perform a miracle in order to teach a lesson, and He cleansed the temple in order to set things right, but Jesus had His power under control. When we are meek, we have that same attitude.

2. Sow Peace. If you stop and think about it, this chapter contains many of the same words Jesus uses in the Sermon on the Mount in Matthew 5. Jesus talked about the blessings of the meek, the pure in heart, and also the peace-makers. Jesus described them as "sons of God" (v. 9). Here, James tells us that wise people actively seek peace; they sow it. That means wise people are constantly working to develop peace between themselves and someone else. The biblical concept of peace is not just being able to tolerate someone or avoiding a major fight. The peace we should seek is a relationship with others that helps us grow closer together and work together for God. This peace values others and encourages all of us to put our personal opinions and preferences on the back-burner and unite through God's Word.

Have you ever known someone who got in an argument and became an entirely different person, an individual who would kick and scream until someone agreed with him? Even when that person was right, you still didn't want to take his side, did you? Let's be honest – at some point, we have all made that mistake. Even when we have to discuss disagreements as a church family, physical family, or youth group, wisdom requires us to do it peacefully. We should never lose our friends for the sake of winning arguments, and we should never make God look bad in an effort to make ourselves look good.

3. Pray for It. Although this piece of advice from James sounds simple enough, it is challenging. Did you notice at the end of verse 5 that James guaranteed this prayer would be answered? Sometimes we pray for things that are outside of God's will for us, but this is one request that God will always grant. If you think about it, there is never a time when it isn't good for us to have more wisdom. We all need it, and no one ever reaches a point when he/she has enough. How much wiser do you think you would be if you prayed for wisdom every day?

Time-Out #4

Read 1 Corinthians 1:18-31. What are some things that God set in place that seem like foolishness to mankind? Are there any things God asks us to do today that might seem foolish? List those as well. Now, take a minute to reflect on why those things are wise, not foolish, and remind yourself that God is ultimately in control.

Putting It All Together

1. Is wisdom the same thing as knowledge? Why or why not?
2. Why is wisdom so important?
3. Can you think of some individuals considered wise by today's standards that practice worldly wisdom?
4. Can you think of some biblical individuals who used God's wisdom to guide their lives?
5. How can we grow in our wisdom?

Taking It Home

Pick out a time of day, and plan to pray for wisdom at that time each day. Be alert for the ways in which God will answer that prayer; there may be events which occur in your life that will teach you wisdom.

Chapter 8

Friend or Enemy?
James 4:1-5

Frenemies

Not so long ago, a new word entered the English vocabulary. It found its way into popular songs and TV shows. The movie *Mean Girls,* released on DVD in the past few years, contained the following conversation between high school students:

> Regina: We do not have a clique problem at this school.
> Gretchen: But you do have to watch out for "frenemies."
> Regina: What are "frenemies"?
> Gretchen: Frenemies are enemies who act like friends. We call them "frenemies."

Since then, the word has become much more common. Celebrities with on-again, off-again feuds have used the word to describe each other. Books written about international politics have described other countries with the term. The business world has begun using it to describe competing co-workers. It seems like a lot of people don't mind having "frenemies," but that term doesn't translate well into our Christian life. According to James, we either choose to be a friend of God or His enemy; there is no middle ground. We don't get to switch back and forth – we have to make the decision to be a friend of God. James tells us how.

The Source of Conflict

By now, it is obvious that the Christians reading this letter were experiencing conflict. If we are honest, all of us experience conflict in our lives. What might not be quite as obvious is the source of that conflict. In chapter 1, James revealed that temptation is often a result of humans being carried away by ungodly desires. Now, he tells them that the conflict that exists among them is also due to those inner desires. Verse 2 shows us that even seemingly harmless thoughts of lust and covetousness can lead to terrible acts, like murder. While that might sound strange to us, maybe even hard to believe, it is important to realize that the ideas behind such terrible reactions all begin somewhere.

Jesus taught this principle in the Sermon on the Mount. Jews knew that the Old Law prohibited murder, but Jesus told them that someone who held anger and resentment toward his brother was just as guilty (Matthew 5:21). Obviously,

Time-Out #1

Break the class up into several small groups. Have each one search the Bible for examples of individuals who had a sinful desire that began in their hearts but led to serious sin. After a few minutes, compare notes to see which group came up with the most examples.

we haven't seen anyone put in jail for murder just for being angry with another person. From a spiritual perspective, Jesus is letting us know how destructive holding on to anger can be. After all, the action of murder often begins with someone holding on to anger and letting it grow. Jesus is just as concerned with our inner thoughts as He is with our outer actions. He also told His hearers that it wasn't enough just to avoid the sexual sin of adultery. They needed to eliminate lust from their lives as well (Matthew 5:27, 28). In fact, Jesus said that someone who looked at a woman in lust had already "committed adultery with her in his heart." Sexual sin doesn't just happen (remember the story of David and Bathsheeba?). It is the result of desires that exist in our heart. Jesus warns us against those desires, and James describes those inner feelings as a source of conflict.

The Result of the Conflict

What was happening as a result of all this conflict? James says that their prayers were not being answered. That sounds pretty harsh doesn't it? James tells us exactly why in verse 3; they wanted to spend God's blessings on their pleasures. We all pray for ourselves from time to time – for health, wisdom to handle life's challenges, etc., but it seems that James's readers took it one step further. They prayed for blessings with the intention to spend them on "their pleasures." They weren't concerned about helping other people. They were concerned about helping themselves by gratifying their desires. Have you ever been tempted to do that in prayer? We can turn on the T.V. and see preachers telling us exactly how God will help us get ahead in life. Is that the right motivation for praying to God?

Over the past few years, a few lines of the Old Testament have gained significant popularity – the prayer of Jabez in 1 Chronicles 4:10. You have probably even seen posters with Jabez's request to God from that verse – "Oh that you would bless me and enlarge my territory!

> **Time-Out #2**
>
> James uses the word "covet" in this passage, and he shows that coveting leads to sin. Is coveting a friend's possession the same thing as admiring it? As a class, brainstorm the difference between coveting something and simply admiring it. How can we avoid falling into the coveting trap?

Let your hand be with me, and keep me from harm so that I will be free from pain." We see from the end of that verse that God granted His request. While entire books have been written about this prayer, we need to remember that we don't know much about Jabez and his life other than what we see in these two verses. It does appear that Jabez honestly asks for God's blessings, and his requests were granted. That should encourage us in prayer, but we need to be careful not to take Jabez's statements out of context. As Christians, we would do well to follow that example and ask God to bless us, but only so we can serve Him. We shouldn't see verses like this one as a license to ask for God's blessings to satisfy our selfish motives. Receiving God's blessings will allow us to share His Word with more people. Enlarging our "territory" will allow us to influence more people with our faith. Staying out of harm's way will let us live a longer life of service to the Lord. We must always remember that when we pray for blessings, it should be out of a desire to serve the One who blesses us, not to serve ourselves.

Choosing Sides

James also tells us that declaring our friendship with the "world" is like saying we are enemies of God. This is a tricky distinction, because two of the most famous verses in Scripture tell us that God created the world (Genesis

56

Time-Out #3

Select a couple of volunteers to participate in a little experiment. Have them leave the room, and then divide the class into two groups. One group will be "friends" with the first volunteer and "enemies" with the second one. Choose these groups at random, and make sure the volunteers don't see who is in which group. When the two come into the room, announce that every person in the class has the job of going to each individual and asking for his/her favorite Bible verse. Everyone will have paper and pencil, ready to pretend that they are participating. Whenever a volunteer approaches a "friend," that person should smile and be extremely helpful. Whenever a volunteer approaches an "enemy," that person should ignore the volunteer and be rude when finally responding. After a few minutes, stop the exercise and see if each volunteer can point out who were the "friends" and who were the "enemies." Even in a setting like this one, we can tell our friends and our enemies by the way they act.

1:1), and He loves the world (John 3:16). The phrase "friendship with the world" here does not mean that we can't have friends who aren't Christians. In fact, if we are going to spread the gospel, we need to build relationships with people who aren't Christians. The point James is making is that our society has different values than Christians should have. If we value what the world loves and try to look, act, and dress just like everyone at school, we are declaring friendship with the world. As God's people, there will be some movies we don't watch, some kinds of clothes we won't wear, and some things we won't say. We can't try to have one foot in both camps in this battle; we must be entirely devoted to God. We already know it is impossible to serve two masters (Luke 16:13), and James reminds us of that fact.

A Different Kind of Temple

James also refers to the spirit God causes to live within us in verse 5. While the reference is not 100% clear, many think that James is referring to the indwelling Holy Spirit. If that is the case, this verse is similar to other statements Paul makes in 1 Corinthians. In 1 Corinthians 3:16, Paul speaks of the church as "God's Temple," where the Holy Spirit lives.

In 1 Corinthians 6:19, Paul refers to the body of a Christian as God's Temple, where the Holy Spirit lives. Both are true, and they should both change our perspective on life. Both the collective life of a church and the individual life of a Christian should be different because of God's presence. The same is true for your youth group – as a group of Christians, God's Spirit lives in you. Does your youth group reflect the Spirit of God?

Putting It All Together

1. Can you think of any blessings that you don't have in your life simply because you haven't thought to ask God for them?

2. Based on what we know about God's love for us and His infinite knowledge, what might we assume if we ask God and do not receive? What are the possible reasons for that?

3. Share some examples of prayer requests that are often asked with the wrong motives.

4. As Christians, how do we love everyone in the world without having a "friendship with the world?"

5. What does it mean to be a true friend? That definition should also be applied to our relationship with God.

Time-Out #4

How does knowing that God's Spirit dwells within us change the way we should live? Make a list of things Christians shouldn't do as a result of God's Spirit living within them.

Taking It Home

Teenagers are a target age group for advertisers and corporations, and many of the commercials we see are based on principles that are far from Christian. Keep your eyes open this week in ads on tv/radio/internet that might be directly contrary to God's will.

Chapter 9

Humble Yourself
James 4:6-12

Pride Comes Before...

While you may not have visited Spain and watched one first-hand, most of us are familiar with the practice of bull-fighting. We've seen pictures and movies about a matador in the ring, usually wearing a brightly colored costume, taunting a charging bull and dodging it at the last possible second. This sport is a big money-maker, with large crowds all pressing in to get a glimpse at the battle – bull vs. matador. Obviously, the sport is dangerous, but there hasn't been a death associated with bull-fighting in over 20 years. The last recorded death of a bull-fighter (as of 2008) took place in 1985.

José Cubero was only 21 years old, but he was already enjoying tremendous popularity in the ring. This rising star was well on his way to being one of the best-known bullfighters, until a fateful battle with a particularly difficult bull. José was talented, however, and he struck the bull several times, finally stabbing his sword into the bull for the deathblow. The bull was already bleeding and stumbling around the arena, so José was sure he had won. He may have won the fight, but he hadn't killed the bull. While José turned to wave to the roaring crowd, the bull staggered to its feet. As José was soaking in the applause, the bull stabbed him through his back and into his heart.

This tragedy took place because, for one minute, he turned his back on his enemy to enjoy the cheers of a crowd. Pride can do the same thing to us. If we aren't careful, we can become so caught up in impressing others and looking good for the crowd that we forget about the sin of pride. It can sneak up on us and stab us in the back. One of the most commonly known proverbs is Proverbs 16:18 – "Pride goes before destruction and a haughty spirit before a fall." In today's lesson, James warns us against letting pride stab us in the back, and he shows us steps we can take to keep that from happening.

#1 - Submit to God

It is no accident that James emphasizes drawing close to God in this passage. The more we focus on God's greatness, the less likely we are to focus on ourselves. This principle is obvious in the writings of Paul. In 1 Corinthians, written early in Paul's ministry, he describes himself as the "least of the apostles" (1 Corinthians 15:9). Later in Paul's ministry, he wrote 1 Timothy and stated that he was the chief of sinners (1:15, 16). In his previous role persecuting Christians, Paul was a proud, up-and-coming Pharisee. It seems that the more time Paul spent in ministry, the more humble he became. The more time we spend strengthening our relationship with God, the better perspective we will have on ourselves.

In these verses, James outlines what we should do to build up our relationship with God. First of all, we need to draw near to God, and He will draw near to us (4:8). As in Jesus' parable of the Prodigal Son in Luke 15, when we decide to come to God, He will run to meet us. Then, he tells his readers "wash your hands, you sinners," imagery that reminds us of the need to clean up our lives if we want to be right with God. We can't claim to be following the God we worship on Sunday if we don't live that way the rest of the week. Haven't you known people who did that? If we are honest, we have probably all fallen into that trap at some point. James also tells us to purify our hearts. It is not enough to go through the motions on the outside; our inner life must be pure as well. This keeps us from being "double-minded," with divided

Time-Out #1

As a class, brainstorm the times when it is most tempting to compromise our Christian faith. What can we do to overcome those temptations?

loyalties, trying to serve both God and the world. Scripture is clear that we can't serve two masters (Matthew 6:24), so we constantly need to be working to make sure our hearts are pure. Lastly, James tells his readers to change their laughter to mourning. In other words, we need to repent of our sins with a clear understanding of the serious nature of sin. This doesn't mean that Christians have to walk around depressed all the time in order to please God. It just means that if we want to maintain a relationship with God, we need to realize the importance of repentance.

#2 - Resist the Devil

When you think of Satan, what comes to your mind? Do you imagine a little costumed character, wearing red and carrying a pitchfork? Cartoons often paint the picture of Satan as a small, mustached creature with a tail who looks fierce but is ultimately harmless. This idea is common, but it is dangerous. When Peter describes Satan, he uses the picture of a lion on the prowl, looking for food (1 Peter 5:8). Does that sound like a cartoon character? Satan is real, and so is the power he possesses. Now, another question: Who is the opposite of Satan? Our first instinct might be God. After all, Satan is determined to do evil and God is holy. We need to be careful, though, because God is not the opposite of Satan in every way; He is far more powerful. We used Job as an example earlier – the first two chapters of the book shows us that Satan has power, but God is ultimately the one in control.

Time-Out #2

We have seen how important it is to have Christian friends to strengthen us against Satan's attacks. In Ecclesiastes 4:12, we read that a cord of three strands is not easily broken. Let's test that theory. Collect some sticks or branches before class (make sure they are not too thick, but bigger than twigs). Have a volunteer break one of the sticks in half. Then, take three of those sticks and tie them tightly together with a rubber band. Have that same volunteer try to break the pile of sticks. How was that different? What does that tell us about our spiritual lives?

The reason we can never lose sight of God's ultimate control is because the only way we can resist Satan is through God's power. Without a relationship with God, we won't be able to stand up under Satan's attacks. James tells us in verse 7 (after reminding us to submit to God), that when we resist Satan, he will flee from us. Peter gives us similar advice in 1 Peter 5:9, stating that resisting Satan means standing firm in our faith, and realizing that we are not alone. Peter's original audience was undergoing some serious persecution, and Peter wanted them to know they weren't the only ones. That same principle holds true for us. Do you ever feel like you are the only one at school who is a Christian? Think about the teens in your school and schools all over your area who are facing the same problems. This is where a youth group can be so encouraging – be sure to find other Christian teens (either in your congregation or at one nearby) that you can hang out with and get to know. The stronger our relationship with God is (not to mention our relationship with other Christians), the better we will be able to resist Satan's attacks.

#3 -Humble Yourself

Someone once said, "In this life, you can choose to exalt yourself, or you can humble yourself. Whatever you do in this life, God will do the opposite in the next." Whoever first made that statement must have been reading this passage, because James stresses the importance of humility over and over again. In verse 6, he refers to a concept we see throughout the Old Testament; God opposes the proud but gives grace to the humble. In verse 10, he makes the statement we sing during devotionals – "Humble yourself in the sight of the Lord and He will lift you up." We might sing that song often, but isn't there more to being humble? How can we increase our humility?

If we are looking for an example of humility, we don't need to look any further than the gospels. No one embodied the life of a servant more than Jesus Christ. Paul tells us that Jesus, who is in very nature God, took on the role of a servant to come to earth (Philippians 2:6, 7). Throughout His ministry, Jesus dealt with Jewish teachers who were obsessed with their status as teachers. They wanted to have all the authority and respect of the people, and they were concerned about praying and giving so that others could see them (Matthew 6:2-8). Jesus showed His followers that true greatness comes by serving. John 13 gives us insight into Jesus' servant attitude, as He washed the apostles' feet.

Washing feet was the task of a common servant in the house. You can probably picture how dirty someone's feet could become walking around dusty roads in sandals all day. This was definitely not a pleasant task. By taking on this task, Jesus was placing Himself in the position of a household servant. At first, Peter was so shocked by this action that he refused to have his feet washed by Jesus (vss. 6-8). After He washed the apostles' feet, Jesus told them to follow His example (vss. 14, 15). Just as He had served them, He wanted them to serve one another. The text says He washed the feet of each apostle, which would include Judas. Later in this chapter, we see that Jesus

Time-Out #3

Bring a large container of water and a rag to class, and select a volunteer to wash a few feet! If your class is small enough, everyone can participate. Nothing fancy is called for, just rinsing off someone's feet and drying them with a towel. Take a few minutes to read John 13. Then, after a few feet have been washed, answer these questions – How did it feel to wash someone else's feet? What would it have been like in the first century, when sandals would have allowed dust and grime to be caked all over someone's feet? Can you imagine Jesus, our Lord, washing feet?

knew Judas would betray Him. Jesus washed the feet of the person He knew would turn Him over to the Jewish authorities. How would it feel to serve someone you knew was already planning to turn on you? The example of humility Jesus left for us includes serving everyone, even our enemies.

#4 - Stop Judging

Have you ever found out that one of your close friends was talking about you behind your back? Do you know that sinking feeling when it seems like everyone in the hallway at school is laughing at you because of something someone said? Can you think of people at your school who used to be best friends until one of them spread a rumor about the other? Gossip has the capability to ruin relationships. The rumors don't have to be true; it hurts just to have someone say something, anything, negative about you. James' readers dealt with the same problem, another reminder of the relevance of God's Word to our lives. He already warned them about the destructive power of the tongue in chapter three, and he follows this discussion of humility with a reminder not to "speak against" each other.

James makes an interesting statement when he says that speaking against someone or judging him is like speaking against or judging God's Law. In other words, when we talk about someone behind his/her back, it is like we are telling God that His Law doesn't matter. After all, if God's Law truly mattered to us, then we wouldn't be breaking it. Have you ever thought about sin this way? The next time you are tempted to talk about someone behind his/her back, remember that you would not only be sinning against someone

Time-Out #4

People are often quick to quote Jesus' words in Matthew 7:1 – "Do not judge, or you will be judged." In verse 12, James reminds his readers not to judge others. Yet, we know that God's Word is designed to correct us when we aren't living right (2 Timothy 3:16). Draw two columns on the board and as a class, brainstorm the differences between judging according to our human standards and allowing ourselves to be judged by God's standards.

else, but against God as well. The best way to show God that we love Him is to respect His Law.

Putting It All Together

1. In this passage, James mentions the attacks of Satan. What are ways that Satan is attacking our world today? Your school? Your youth group?

2. Which do you think our society values more – pride or humility? Why?

3. Can you think of any biblical individuals who showed great humility?

4. In what areas of your life is it easy to become full of pride?

5. What are some specific ways we can grow in our humility?

Taking It Home

This week, be on the lookout for a chance to stand against gossip (what James calls "slander") at school. Choose one time this week when you can do just the opposite and spread something good about someone else to all your friends. Try to "talk good" about people behind their backs!

Chapter 10

Life is Short
James 4:13-17

Did You Know These Facts About Human Life?

Tom Heymann, author of *In An Average Lifetime*, has reported that the average human being spends…

- 3 years in business meetings.
- 13 years watching TV.
- $89,281 on food.
- Consumes 109,354 pounds of food.
- Makes 1811 trips to McDonalds.
- Spends $6881 in vending machines.
- Eats 35,138 cookies and 1483 pounds of candy.
- Catches 304 colds.
- Is involved in 6 motor vehicle accidents.
- Is hospitalized 8 times (men) or 12 times (women).
- Spends 24 years sleeping.
- *Here's one last fact about human life – it won't last forever! It is important that we use it wisely.*

Where Are You Headed?

Chances are, you have already thought about your future: where you want to go to college, what line of work is right for you, etc. What is the basis for making those decisions? When choosing a college, are you looking for a place where you can grow spiritually, or a school that your friends think is cool? When settling on a career, will you look for a line of work that allows you to serve God the best, or a job that will pay the best? It is not wrong to go to a university your friends like, and it is not a sin to have a high-paying job, but we need to examine our priorities when deciding those things. Over the next few years, you are going to make choices that will affect the rest of your life.

That isn't meant to scare anyone, just to remind us all that when it comes to decision-making, spiritual priorities should always trump physical concerns. In 4:13-17, James is dealing with that same issue.

What Is Our Top Priority?

The first problem James addresses is the planning certain individuals had done. Obviously, it is not unchristian to plan for the future. One of Jesus' teachings reminds us of this fact. In the last few verses of Luke 14, Jesus wanted His followers to consider the cost of following Him. In verses 28-30, Jesus describes how foolish it would be for one of them to decide to build a tower without first stopping to think how much it would cost. If the foundation were completed without anything else being built, the builder would be the laughingstock of the entire community. In verses 31-33, Jesus reminded the crowd that before starting a war, a king should sit down to discover whether he has enough soldiers. If he didn't, then he would need to strike a peace treaty before the fighting began. God blesses us with common sense, and He wants us to use it.

Time-Out #1

Take a minute as a class for each individual to write down his/her goals for the next ten years. Try to come up with at least five major objectives you want to accomplish. Pick one to share with the rest of the group. Now, think through each of your goals; how will you be able to glorify God in accomplishing them? If there is something you want to do with your life that won't leave room for God, you might want to rethink it.

James is not angry that they are planning out their lives; he is upset that they have left God out of the equation. Interestingly, the Greek term for "carry on business" that James uses here is found only one other place in the entire New Testament. Peter uses the term in 2 Peter 2:3 to talk about greedy people who lie in order to exploit others. It seems that these individuals have allowed business to become their number one priority. They were making business decisions and confidently telling each other what was going to happen next without even thinking about what God would want. In verse 16, we find out they are bragging about how much money they were making and what they were accomplishing. James told them it was sinful to brag in that way, as if God wasn't ultimately in control.

The first step in learning how to improve our decision making is to realize *serving God must be a Christian's top priority*. Do you remember the first of the ten commandments given in the Old Testament? The first one God mentions is that His people should have no other gods before them (Exodus 20:3). Just a quick glance at the Old Testament shows us what a challenge this commandment was for Israel. One of their biggest temptations was to begin serving the false gods of the nations around them. Even when Jesus walked the earth, He dealt with Pharisees and scribes who were more concerned about their own authority than following God's Son. God has always wanted serving Him to be our #1 priority, and when we lose sight of that fact, our lives can quickly unravel.

Who Is Really In Control?

James is quick to point out the reason we shouldn't make plans as if we are the ones in control – we aren't. In verse 14, James reminds us that we cannot even predict what will happen tomorrow. How many times has a quick storm shown up that meteorologists didn't expect? How many underdog sports teams have we watched succeed against all expert predictions? The truth is, none of us can foresee what will happen five minutes from now, much less a few days or weeks from now. No matter how many plans we make, nothing is guaranteed.

Jesus brought that point home in a parable Luke records in Luke 12:15-21.

Time-Out #2

Steven Covey made this illustration famous in his book *First Things First*, and it is a great way to show the importance of priorities. You'll need a large, wide-mouthed jar (it can be glass or plastic, just as long as it is transparent), as well as a few large rocks, some gravel, sand, and water. The goal is to get the rocks, gravel, sand, and water into the jar. What is the best way to do it? Should you put the sand in first? What if you poured in the water before doing anything else? The only way it is possible to fit everything in is to put the big rocks in first, then the gravel, the sand, and the water. It can all fit, but the "big rocks" need to be in place. Serving God is the "big rock" in our lives that must be in place before we add anything else.

He spoke of a man whose harvest was so great one year that he didn't have enough room to store his crops. His solution was to tear down his barns and build bigger ones to store all his grain. Then, he could kick back, take it easy, and rely on what he has stored. That sounds like a good plan, right? Not according to Jesus. The story ends with God demanding this man's soul. He was prepared for retirement, but not for eternity.

That seems like a harsh reaction, doesn't it? After all, what is wrong with storing up crops for future use? In verse 21, Jesus points to the real reason this man was punished. He was storing things up for himself without thinking of how to please God. He was so focused on securing His own future that he forgot to serve God, who was in control of the future. When we make plans as if we only have to rely on ourselves, we do the same thing. It is easy to think, like the rich man, that we are in control of our own destinies. When things go well, we think, "I've done a great job with my life," or "I've made a lot of money," and we forget that God is ultimately the source of all good gifts (remember James 1:17?).

The second step in learning how to make decisions is to understand *we are not in control.* The rich man couldn't predict his future, and we can't predict ours. To remind us of this fact, James tells us to say "If the Lord wills," before we state what we will be doing in the future. You have probably heard people begin or end a sentence by saying, "Lord willing." That is more than just a simple phrase, it is a constant reminder that God is in control. It also encourages us to begin our planning by seeking God's will in prayer. Have you ever decided what you were going to do and then prayed for God to bless the decision you had already made? When we understand that God is in control, prayer time is the first stop, not the last stop, when we are making plans.

How Much Time Do We Have?

Probably the most haunting illustration in the entire book of James is found in verse 14. James tells us that our life is a mist that exists for a while, and then fades into thin air. While that word picture is not fun to think about, it is true. Think about it – you have never met someone who lived forever. It is easy, especially when we are young, to feel invincible, as if nothing will ever slow us down. If we are honest, we know that isn't true. Believe it or not, James did not share that fact to depress us, but to remind us of what is important. Since life does not last forever, we need to invest our time and energy into what *will* last forever. Remember the man who built bigger barns? Do you think he was allowed to take all of his crops with him into eternity? Of course not, and we won't take anything physical with us.

The third step when making life decisions is to *focus on what really matters.* Take this quick test: What is the last problem that really frustrated you? Was it a comment made by a friend? An unfair assignment from a teacher? A complaint by your parents? In comparison to eternity, where does the importance of that problem rank? Most of the challenges we face and frustrations we complain about pale in comparison to what truly matters. The next time you are upset, check to make sure that your problem passes the "eternity test."

> ### Time-Out #3
> Bring an aerosol can of air freshener or hairspray to class. Spray it in the air and watch it evaporate. Take a minute to reflect on how that symbolizes our short lives in comparison to eternity. What should that teach us about how we act in this life?

What Should We Do?

The last step for making the right decisions is tucked away in verse 17: *Do what you know is right.* James tells us that refusing to do something we know we should is a sin. In the context, James is telling his readers that since they now know how to make plans God's way, they need to do it. Since James has corrected them, they now have no excuse. The same is true for us as we study God's Word. The more we learn about God's will for our lives, the greater responsibility we have to follow it. Remember James's encouragement to be "doers" of the Word? That means we can't ignore our responsibility to be nice to the teens in our youth group who are often left out by everyone else. We can't ignore the quiet time with God we know

> ### Time-Out #4
> As a class, take a second to brainstorm this question: What are some things we know we should do but are often tempted not to? Make a list on the board and think through each one. What are some ways you can overcome that temptation and avoid the sin James teaches about in verse 17?

is important. We can't ignore our obligation to do our own work, even when all of our friends are cheating. Once we have put God first, realized He is in control, and focused on what really matters, we have to follow through by acting on what we know.

Putting It All Together

1. What are some of your goals in life that will honor God?
2. Name a few goals that are popular with the world, but don't honor God.
3. What is the criteria for a choice that honors God?
4. What is the difference between saving up our money, resources, etc. and hoarding our possessions like the man who built bigger barns?
5. Can you think of some common problems that often bother us that wouldn't pass the "eternity test"?

Taking It Home

Before you do anything this week, stop and think about James's word picture of life as a mist. That might change the way we view even the most mundane day. We only have a limited amount of time to make an impact with our lives.

Chapter 11

Rich & Famous...and About to Be Miserable
James 5:1-6

Our society is obsessed with celebrities. We want to know who they are dating, where they are eating, and how much they are making. We try to look like them, dress like them, and be like them. We talk about them on a first name basis, as if we are close personal friends! If we want to inject some energy into a game show or reality show, we put together a "Celebrity Edition." We vote by the thousands to determine which celebrity dances better than the others, and hundreds of thousands line up every year to audition for shows that give them a chance to perform, lose weight, or compete with other contestants to win someone's heart. What do they want? The chance to become a celebrity.

To illustrate our country's obsession with "celebrity worship," I want to share a memory from an episode of *Entertainment Tonight* (I know, it sounds weird to reference *ET* to make a spiritual point, but go with me). I had just returned from a six-week mission trip to Bangkok, Thailand, and I stayed up until midnight talking to my family about everything that had happened. We spent our time in Thailand teaching conversational English to college students, using the book of Luke. A few of our students took us to one of Bangkok's most famous tourist attractions – the Emerald Buddha. As we looked at this green image of Buddha, I saw a scene that was burned into my mind from that day forward. The room was full of Thai citizens bowing down before this statue, worshiping Buddha. I was sitting on the couch at home, with this memory replaying in my mind after everyone else had gone to bed. The time zone difference and jet lag kept me wide awake, so I turned on the TV. Do you know what the lead story was on *Entertainment Tonight*? ET correspondents interviewed people who were at a restaurant where Arnold Schwartzenegger had eaten that weekend. They asked other guests what meal he ordered, how much of it he left on the plate, and they even interviewed the cook about how he prepared the dish. Of all the possible newsworthy items in the country that night, the most important event was that a celebrity had dinner at a restaurant. That's when it hit me – we might not bow down before a green statue, but our country has formed its own god – celebrity.

Let me go ahead and admit it – I do watch a few of the shows mentioned earlier, and some of them are funny and entertaining. Obviously, it is not a sin to watch TV (although there are definitely shows and movies on TV that Christians should avoid), but we need to look carefully at the world of entertainment, because it reveals something about ourselves. Since we have exalted celebrities to such a powerful place in our culture, we often want to be one of them. We dream about the garage full of cars, the theater room, the expensive clothes, and yet we fail to realize that the rich and famous are often rich and miserable. A life of wealth can be a life of emptiness, and it is that emptiness James discusses in chapter 5.

Time-Out #1

Make a list on the board of celebrities that our society seems to worship. Once you have a few written down, stop for a second and think about their lives. What kind of example do they set? Have they ever been in trouble with the law? Has our country seen them undergo serious struggles (divorce, rehab, etc.)? Reflect as a class on the example often set by celebrities, as well as the problems they face. Would you really want to trade places with one of them?

Living the Good Life?

What would you do if you had a bank account full of money, acres of land, and a closet full of expensive clothes? Laugh, shout for joy, faint? James captures the attention of every reader by saying that those who are rich needed to do exactly the opposite – they needed to cry. James mentions the clothes the rich owned (verse 2), the silver and gold they possessed (verse 3), and the fields that belonged to them (verse 4). If you read through the Old and New Testament, you see that clothing, money, and land were the main status symbols of ancient days. If you wanted to find a rich person, you wouldn't look for a fancy car; you would look for a large plot of land. James is clearly angry at these people; did you notice that although he wrote this letter to the "brethren" (1:2), he is calling this group "you rich" (5:1)? He has transitioned from brotherly encouragement to some serious correction.

Why was James so upset? Is it sinful to be rich? The Bible has a lot to say about money. Even in the Old Testament, God wanted His people to take care of the poor. Check out Deuteronomy 15:4-11 as an example. God told the Israelites that there should be no poor people among them, because they were supposed to take care of those in need. The Israelites were not perfect (that sounds like us, doesn't it?), but God's plan was for no one to go hungry or thirsty. James has already told us that the rich were taking people to court needlessly, and that poor people who entered a worship assembly were sometimes judged or ignored. Those actions don't begin to resemble the kindness God wanted His nation to show the poor.

Wealth is mentioned in the New Testament as well, and Jesus addressed it often throughout His ministry. While Jesus walked the earth, many around Him believed wealth was a reward for faithfulness. They thought rich people must be more faithful than others, because their wealth was a gift from God. So in Luke 18, when Jesus meets a

Time-Out #2

Even though Jesus said it was hard for the wealthy to inherit the kingdom of God, He also reminded His followers that anything was possible with God. In order to equip us to handle our riches righteously, God placed several important teachings on money in the New Testament. Here are a few; read them out loud as we focus on wealth.

Hebrews 13:5, 6
1 Timothy 6:6-10
1 Timothy 6:17-19

young, rich man who stated he had faithfully kept God's commandments, he seems like the perfect model of faithfulness. Yet, when he asks Jesus what he should do, Jesus tells him to sell all he has and give it to the poor. The man walks away sadly, because he could not bear to part with his riches (Luke 18:23). Jesus then said it would be easier for a camel to go through the eye of a needle than for a rich person to inherit the kingdom of God (vs. 25). This statement shocked the apostles, because they were used to the thought of riches equaling righteousness. Jesus reveals something important: we need to be willing to sacrifice anything in order to serve God. Our wealth should never stand in our way. The reason it is a challenge for the rich to inherit the kingdom of God is because the more we have, the easier it is for us to be distracted from what is truly important. James is dealing with people who have become so blinded by their wealth they were no longer concerned with how they treat others.

The Problem – Letting Wealth Get in the Way

James was upset with these people because they had misused their wealth. Notice the different actions he mentions: they had hoarded up their money and refused to share it with others (vs. 3), they had failed to pay their workers (vs. 4), they had lived in self-indulgence (vs. 5), and they had condemned and murdered innocent men (vs. 6). Failing to pay workers is also a serious offense. In Luke 10:7, Jesus specifically states that a worker deserves his wages. James 5:6 is challenging to understand, since we don't know exactly what was happening to James' readers. It may be that by denying workers their pay, they were literally condemning them to die without

Time-Out #3

Break up into two groups, and discuss how to approach the following people:

1. Your friend Matt sits down by you at lunch. You aren't to excited, because all he ever talks about is his new truck. Unless he is talking about the new sound system he put in his truck, or the new car his dad bought. You know there is nothing wrong with his truck; in fact, it is really nice, but his obsession with it isn't healthy. What are some ways you can steer the conversation toward something else and remind Matt that money (and his truck, for that matter) isn't everything?

2. Your older sister Sarah has stopped coming to Bible class with your family. She still manages to make it to Sunday morning service (most of the time), but she seems to spend the entire weekend working. Most of your friends have part-time jobs, and you have been thinking about applying for one, but Sarah works all the time. She says it is because she has to pay for going shopping with her friends and going out at night, but she isn't spending any time with your physical family or your church family. What are some ways you can help her see God's priorities?

money to pay for food. Clearly, the way we use our wealth is important to God.

The Solution – Using God's Wealth God's Way

It is possible to be faithful and wealthy at the same time; in fact, there are several people in the Bible who had both riches and faith. Joseph was someone who constantly served God, but also suffered for it. He was sold into slavery and later thrown in prison, but through God's power, Joseph was made Pharaoh's second-in-command. Pharaoh gave him a signet ring, fine robes, and put him in charge of "the whole land of Egypt" (Genesis 47:41-43). Because Joseph was faithful, God was able to use him to save lives during a great famine. Job was an upright, faithful man (Job 1:1), and he owned land, flocks, servants, and was called the "greatest man in the east" (1:3). Satan took away everything and everyone Job held; all Job had left was his wife, a few friends who weren't much help in the comfort department, and his own life. Although the book is filled with the tough questions Job asked, he ultimately remained faithful. At the end, he was blessed with more land, more cattle, and even more children (42:12-15).

Even in the New Testament, we find wealthy individuals who served God. Jesus meets Zacchaeus in Luke 19, and Zacchaeus is a wealthy man. He is a tax-collector, so he wasn't the most well-liked person in the world, but he did have a great deal of money. In fact, Jesus goes to Zaccaheus's house to eat. While he is there, Zacchaeus reveals that he has cheated some people (which was common for the tax-collectors of that day), and he wanted to pay them back four times what he took (19:8). As if that wasn't enough, he decided to give half his possessions to the poor. Acts 16:14, 15 introduces us to Lydia, a seller of purple. Purple was a color usually associated with royalty, and those who sold it were producing material used by kings. Not only was Lydia a seller in this elite business, she had a home large enough to invite everyone over after she obeyed the gospel.

What is the difference, then? What makes these individuals different from the rich condemned by James? You probably noticed that although the above individuals were wealthy, they used their wealth to serve the Lord – giving to the poor, showing hospitality, etc. It is not a sin to be rich; it is a sin to be rich and refuse to use God's blessings to serve God's purpose. James is dealing with people who had done just that, and we should continually pray that God will give us strength to avoid that trap.

Which Riches Are More Important?

We should take this passage as a serious warning about wealth. You may notice many times when rich people are mentioned in the Bible, it is because they are sinning. Many of the times we read about poor people, they are faithful. As we have pointed out, that is not always true, but the Bible is clear that physical wealth often distracts people from serving God. Even if we don't feel like we are rich, we live in a wealthy country, and there is always the danger of our stuff blinding us to what really matters. So, just because wealth isn't inherently sinful, don't forget that it does bring with it temptations. We need to be careful. James paints a clear picture of the misery waiting on people who put earthly wealth above living righteously – let's not make the same mistake.

James teaches that wealth is only temporary – clothes eventually become moth-eaten, while gold and silver corrode. In the same way, cars eventually rust, videogame systems become outdated, mp3 players break, because none of them will last forever. Jesus taught about the inheritance that won't be destroyed by moth and rust – treasures in heaven (Matthew 6:20). If we focus on serving God more than collecting stuff, we can choose to build up riches in heaven rather than wealth on earth.

Putting It All Together
1. What are some things money can buy?
2. What are some things money can't buy?

3.   Name a few of the ways the media tells us we should spend our money.

4.   Why do you think we are so tempted to misuse our money?

5.   Is there anything about the way you spend your money that you want to change after reading this passage?

Taking It Home

When you watch TV this week, try to find the not-so-hidden messages advertisers put in shows and commercials. What are they communicating?

Chapter 12

Hold On!
James 5:7-12

The Endurance of *Endurance*

On August 8, 1914, a ship named "Endurance" left port in Plymouth, England for the Antarctic. At the helm was Ernest Shackleton, an explorer whose bravery made him well-known. This was during a time when it seemed like everyone was interested in Antarctica, and Ernest had already been on several expeditions. As he and his crew made their way into that frigid area, they arrived just in time for winter conditions. The ship became frozen in an ice floe in the Weddell Sea. The only choice they had was to wait until warmer weather in the spring. When the ice began to melt, however, it did more damage to the ship. By the time October of 1915 rolled around, the crew had to abandon their home for the last year, which was slowly but surely sinking, having been torn apart by the ice.

As if that wasn't bad enough, the next leg of their trip consisted of camping out on an ice floe, in hopes that it would drift toward a nearby island. In December, they thought the weather might be cold enough for the ice to have frozen between their location and the island, so that they could trudge through the icy slush. That didn't work, however, so they had to set up another camp, which they named *Patience*. Would you have had any patience left at this point? All they could do was trust that the current would take them toward the island, and it did. They were only 60 miles away from Paulet Island, when they realized that the ice between them in the island was impossible to navigate. Even worse, on April 9th, the ice floe which held their camp broke in two. Their last resort was to enter into the lifeboats they had been saving and hope they could find land. After a week at sea in lifeboats, they landed on Elephant Island.

Shackleton's story is fascinating, and some historians have referred to it as the "most successful failure" in the history of explorers. As you read about all the trials they faced, what stands out above everything else was their perseverance. They were able to hold on, no matter what was going on around them. Sure, they had to leave their boat, their plans were constantly being ruined by weather, and they had to spend months in freezing temperatures, but they held on and eventually persevered. As we have seen in earlier passages, James's readers were suffering for their faith. While we don't know all the details, we know they must have been getting discouraged (wouldn't you?). As James continues chapter 5, he encourages them to "hold on," and he tells them how.

Hold On To Your Patience

In verses 7 and 8, James stresses the value of patience. We live in a world that is not very patient. We e-mail instead of writing letters, and if we need an answer right away, we send a text message instead of an e-mail. We order pizza that is guaranteed to be delivered soon, and we heat up leftover slices in the microwave. One recent commercial showed a man buying a new TV, and the song in the background was blaring, "I want it all, and I want it now." That describes the current culture pretty well, but James tells us that shouldn't describe Christians. His readers needed to be patient as they waited for the coming of the Lord. Remember, God's timing is not our timing. Peter tells us in 2 Peter 3:8, that with God one day is like a thousand years, and a thousand years is like a day. To us, it seems like the Lord's return has taken a long time, but that isn't true from God's perspective. In fact, from His viewpoint, it has only been a couple of days! Verse 9 goes on to explain that while God isn't slow in keeping His promise, He is patiently waiting since He wants all people to come to Him.

James uses the image of a farmer to describe patience, and that brings up an important aspect of waiting on God's timing. Farmers are patient, waiting on their land to produce crops, but that doesn't mean they are lazy. A farmer can't just sit around and hope for a good harvest. Among other things, he has to prepare the soil, plant the crops, maintain and fertilize so they will be in good condition, and constantly defend the fields from pests that could ruin the crops. A farmer is patient, but he is still active. He does the work he knows is necessary and then patiently waits for the rains to come. In our lives, we can't let the pursuit of patience turn into laziness. Our goal as Christians is not to simply sit around and wait for the Lord to return; we have to be active. Paul dealt with a similar mindset when he wrote the Thessalonian church. Some of those Christians were apparently so excited about the Lord's coming that they quit their jobs and weren't working. In 2 Thessalonians 3, Paul reminds them that they didn't learn that from him. When he was with the congregation there, he was working hard. In verse 12, he urges them to "settle down and earn the bread they eat." Being truly patient and waiting for God does not give us permission to be lazy. In fact, it does just the opposite – it motivates us to work for the Lord.

Hold On To a Good Attitude

After telling us to be patient, James goes on to explain that we shouldn't "grumble against" one another. While we probably don't use that same language, we all deal with that temptation don't we? One year, at our congregation's summer camp, we began the week by reading Philippians 2:14 – "Do everything without grumbling or complaining…" Our challenge was to go through the entire week without complaining. Any time someone was overheard complaining about the cold showers or the hot weather, nearby campers would call them on it. Our youth minister even came up with his own "buzzer" sound effect that he would use whenever he heard someone grumbling. Do you know what we noticed? Sometimes, we complain without even realizing it. We also experienced one of the best weeks of Summer Camp we had ever had, and I am convinced it was because we tried our best to eliminate complaining. What would your school be like if complaining was completely eliminated? What if grumbling was totally banned from your youth group? What would that look like?

> **Time-Out #1**
>
> The world of farming would have been a part of daily life for James's audience, but it might not be as familiar to us. To illustrate patience, why not plant some seeds in dirt in a large clay pot that you can leave in the classroom? You can even write out James 5:7 across the pot itself, and once the plant blooms, you will have a constant reminder of James' instructions about patience.

He also links the way we "grumble" against our brothers and sisters with judgment. We know Jesus taught that the judgment we used toward others is the same judgment we will receive (Matthew 7:2). When He offered the model prayer, Jesus also reminded His followers that the way they forgave others directly affected how they were forgiven (Matthew 6:15). James wanted his audience to keep in mind the eternal implications of mistreating each other. He uses this phrase in verse 9 – "The Judge is standing at the door!" Have you ever seen the behavior of a small child change when his mother walks in the room? Or maybe you have noticed an entire classroom run to their desks and sit quietly when they hear the teacher walking down the hallway. James wants us to know that God, our Judge, see us, and we need to live that way. Since we know God wants what is best for us (like a parent or a teacher), that shouldn't be a scary thought. It should, however, encourage us to live like He would want us to live.

Hold On To Godly Examples

In order to help his readers stand firm and persevere, James points them to Old Testament examples. The average Jew would have heard these stories from birth. The prophets were especially important for the Jewish people. Sometimes, prophets would suffer as a result of the Israelites' sin. For example, Ezekiel was commanded by God to lie on his left side for 390 days, then on his right side for 40 days (Ezekiel 4:4-6). Have you ever gotten sore from falling asleep in a weird position? Can you imagine how sore it would be to lie on your side for over a year? Often, the prophets were ignored and mistreated by God's own people – the very people they were sent to reach. Shortly before his death, Stephen reminded the Sanhedrin that the Jews always found a way to persecute the prophets (Acts 7:52).

James also includes Job in this list of examples. Earlier, we touched on Job's story of suffering. When compared with Job's tragic misfortune, all of our problems seem pretty insignificant. As you review Job's story, there is one

Time-Out #2

As a class, brainstorm this question: If you had just one week left before your life was over, what would you do? Make a list on the board of everything you would want to accomplish. Now, ask the same question with a slight change – what if you had just one day left? When James wrote, he understood something we all need to remember: Jesus could come at any time. That is why he states that the Lord's coming is near (vs. 8). How will living as if Jesus could return any minute change our lives?

Time-Out #3

Time for everyone's favorite old-school children's game — Simon Says! Take a few minutes and play a quick game of Simon Says in your class. After you have a winner, discuss what makes the game a challenge. Usually, the leader can trick people by asking them to do something, but making a different motion himself. The reason that works so often is because what we do usually comes across more strongly than what we say. The prophets were willing not just to speak in God's name, but to live God's way. If we want to follow their example, we need to do the same.

aspect that seems strange. When God appears to Job and speaks from the whirlwind, He never explains why Job was suffering. If you read the first two chapters of the book of Job, it is obvious why all of that happened to him. Wouldn't it have been easy for God to explain everything to him? Yet, God asks Job to trust Him simply because He is God and Job is not. Since Job does just that, he receives his reward. We may experience events that we don't understand, and God calls us to trust Him anyway. Even if our reward doesn't come until we enter into eternity, our trust will be well worth it. Job's example helps us remember that. The next time you experience pain for being a Christian, some of these examples might just be what you need to hold on and make it through.

Hold On To Your Word

In this passage, James tags on verse 12 as a reminder of what a Christian's speech should sound like. He tells them not to swear an oath by heaven or by earth. He has already warned about the dangers of a tongue that is out of control, and this statement is yet another reminder of how important it is for Christians to speak wisely. Does James's warning mean that a Christian is not allowed to take an oath when testifying in a trial? A closer look at Jesus' final days shows that He answered the high priest while under oath (Matthew 26:64). We also read about oaths before the Lord in Hebrews 6:16, and the author doesn't teach against them. The kinds of oaths that were common at this time weren't oaths in a courtroom or promises before God. They were the kinds of oaths that were so common there was even a distinction made between binding and non-binding oaths. Here, James tells us that Christians should constantly tell the truth. We don't need to take oaths when we talk to others. They should know by the life that we live we aren't lying to them. When you give people your word, can they trust it? If you are a Christian, the answer should be yes.

Putting It All Together

1. What are some aspects of Christianity that test our patience?

2. What do Christians today need to stand firm against?

3. What are the most common reasons people "grumble against each other" in your youth group? What about your congregation?

4. Can you think of other passages that prove God is full of compassion and mercy?

5. Why is it important for Christians to "let their yes be yes and their no be no?"

Taking It Home

This week, we discussed Old Testament examples of perseverance. During the week, see if you can find a biblical individual who persevered that was not mentioned in class. Jot down the person and biblical reference and compare notes next time.

Time-Out #4

James points to Job as example of endurance. Divide the class up into two teams, and give each team the following assignment. They have to search Scripture to find another biblical example of someone who suffered but persevered. After both teams have spent some time working on their answer, have a spokesperson from each team tell everyone the name of the person they discovered, the way that person persevered, and how that lesson can apply to our lives.

Chapter 13

Our Most Powerful Weacon

Our Most Powerful Weapon

James 5:13-20

"Why is he running for student government? He doesn't have a prayer."

"She hustles after the loose ball, comes up with it, and throws up a prayer at the buzzer…"

"The doctors said there is nothing else they can prescribe. I guess the only thing for us to do now is pray."

What do those statements tell you about prayer? The first one connects prayer to an incredibly unlikely event – not only does the candidate not have a chance, he doesn't even have a prayer. The second sentence equates prayer with a last-ditch effort which isn't very likely to work. She is hurrying to get the ball out of her hands, and it probably won't go in, so rather than being a "shot," it becomes a "prayer." The third statement isn't necessarily wrong – it is always good for us to pray for those who are sick – but did you notice that it assumes that prayer is a kind of "last resort" which isn't nearly as powerful as the work of a doctor?

In today's society, prayer is discussed, debated, and tolerated, but it is rarely respected for its power. In fact, if we are honest, there have probably been times in our lives when we have limited the power of God in our minds by discounting the importance of prayer. While visiting a woman in the hospital one day, I asked what our congregation could do to help her. She responded, "Pray for me – that is the first thing we should do, the last thing we can do, and the best thing we can do." She was absolutely right. Prayer is a powerful weapon, not a last resort, and James reminds us of this fact.

Prayer That Is Powerful

Prayer is one area of Christian life that seems to be a challenge for many of us. Many times, when given the choice of topics for a class or sermon,

Christians put prayer high on the list. We wonder how to pray, what we should pray for, and how we can grow in our prayer life. James closes his book by addressing these issues. In this passage, James teaches three important principles of prayer. To make it easy to remember, just think of the kinds of prayers to pray, the kind of prayer that is heard, and how to become a person of prayer.

The Kinds of Prayers to Pray

First, we pray when we are in trouble (vs. 13). This is a kind of prayer we are familiar with: the prayer you whisper to yourself when a teacher hands out a test and you know you haven't studied, the prayer that flashes through your mind when you are caught in an embarrassing situation. The terminology in this verse refers to any kind of difficulty, so we are reminded that we can pray in any challenging circumstance. It might give us a new perspective to think about the suffering encountered by New Testament Christians. First century Christians were often persecuted for their beliefs, and James has already told us that rich individuals were dragging them into court and apparently exploiting them. They were dealing with serious challenges, which might make some of our problems seem trivial in comparison.

Secondly, we pray when we are happy (vs. 13). This may be one of the most challenging times for us to remember to pray. When things are going badly in our lives, it is much easier to realize our weakness and go to God in prayer. When we feel self-sufficient and confident, it is usually more difficult for us to remember that what we have isn't due to our hard work, but God's blessing. The children of Israel in the Old Testament illustrate this principle over and over again. Just flip through the pages of Judges and look at how many times

Israel lost sight of God when everything was going well. God would allow another nation to take them captive, they would realize their need for God, and they would cry out Him. James urges us to continue to remember God in the good times.

Thirdly, we pray when we are sick (vs. 14). One glance at the prayer list in our congregations shows that we have this in common with James's readers: people we love get sick. You probably know several people right now who are struggling with health problems. Even though we know that this life is only temporary, James reminds us that God cares about our health and listens to our prayers. Verse 14 spells out a specific scenario for those who are suffering with illness. James suggests that they call the elders of the church to pray over them and anoint them with oil. While that first step may seem familiar to us, that last part might cause us to do a double-take. Why were they anointed with oil? Should we do that today? Here's where a little knowledge of James's culture will help us.

Time-Out #2

Take a copy of *Foxe's Book of Martyrs* (it might be available in your church library; if not, you might invest in a copy) and read a few of the powerful stories of early Christian martyrs. How do those accounts make you feel? Do you think we are ever tempted to complain too much about the challenges of Christian life today?

There a couple of different purposes we see for the use of anointing in Scripture. The first, and most likely in this case, is medicinal in nature. Do you remember the parable of the Good Samaritan? When the Samaritan stops to pick up the man who was robbed and left for dead, verse 34 tells us that the Samaritan used oil and wine to bandage his wounds. History has preserved a quote from a famous doctor that lived in the second century, named Galen. He stated that oil was the best treatment for paralysis. This leads us to believe that anointing with oil was like giving medicine to a patient.

Another way we see anointing used in the Bible is to set something apart. In the Old Testament, when Samuel was setting apart David to be king, he anointed him with oil (1 Samuel 16). It is possible that this anointing was a way that culture would set apart someone for special consideration. Either way, James's recommendation is that the elders pray for those who are sick and provide both medicinal and loving care for them. Can you think of anyone in your congregation who has been in the hospital or nursing home for a long time? Even if you aren't an elder, your visit will be a true encouragement to them, and as James reminds us, your prayers will be a true blessing.

Lastly, we pray when we have sinned (vss. 15, 16). In verse 15, James tells us that those who have sinned can be forgiven, and verse 16 spells out how that can happen. Have you ever wondered why sermons often conclude with the opportunity for someone to respond with a request for prayer? There is power when God's people confess sins to each other and pray. This can be especially powerful for a youth group. Is your group a safe place for your friends to share their struggles and sins, or are most people afraid that they will be made fun of or looked at differently because of sharing that kind of personal information? Try to think of some ways you can encourage the kind of caring support in your group that will allow these times of confession.

The Kind of Prayer That Is Heard

Now we know what to pray for, but how do we know that our prayers work? Have you ever had the feeling that your prayers didn't rise any further than the ceiling? When we read about individuals who prayed in the Bible, it is easy to be intimidated. After all, Joshua prayed, and God made the sun stand still (Joshua 10:13, 14). I don't know about you, but nothing that miraculous has ever happened when I prayed! James mentions Elijah praying for it to stop raining (which it did) and praying for it to rain again (which it did – 1 Kings 18:41-45). What was Elijah's secret to such powerful prayer? In verse 17, James points out that Elijah was just a human being, like we are. We sometimes study Bible char-

Time-Out #3

According to recent research by Indiana University, approximately 90% of those surveyed pray on a more or less regular basis, and 60% pray at least once a day. Which of the four categories of prayer do you think is most common among those who pray? Which is least common? As a class, brainstorm a scenario in which you would use each of these four kinds of prayers.

acters as if they are superheroes who always knew how to act and never struggled with maintaining faith, but that isn't true. Elijah was a real person, with real emotions, challenges, and difficulties. Yet, he was powerfully effective in prayer, because he embodied the description in verse 16. He was a righteous man.

The key to powerful and effective prayer is not using big words or sounding "spiritual" in front of other people; the secret is to live a righteous life that pleases God. The way we live affects the way we pray. In fact, Peter wrote to the early church about this principle. In 1 Peter 3:7, Peter tells husbands they need to treat their wives respectfully, so that "nothing will hinder their prayers." In verse 12, he reminds them that God listens to the prayer of the righteous. In 4:7, he urges them to think clearly and practice self-control, "so they can pray." Before we pray about something important to us, we might need to examine our lives. What kinds of sins might keep us from having an effective prayer life? What can we do to avoid those temptations?

The Kind of Christian Who Cares

James ends this discussion of prayer with a couple of verses emphasizing the kinds of concern Christians should have for each other. Not only should we pray for people when they are sick, we should also pray for them when they have fallen away from the church. In fact, if we can bring someone back into the family of God, that person will be saved from death, as well as saved from the sins that were committed. In any church family, it can be easy to lose track of those who are wrestling with spiritual challenges.

This also has a specific application for youth groups or Bible classes in your congregation. You can probably think of people you used to hang out with all the time when the youth group got together that don't come to many youth activities these days. You can probably even picture where they used to sit in Bible class, although they haven't been there lately. When Paul wrote about this problem in Galatians 6:1, he told the Galatian Christians to be gentle when bringing back people who are caught in sin. This isn't a chance to tell the person how wrong they have been and what they should be doing, but to gently bring them back. Maybe you could tell them how much you have missed hanging out with them. It might be helpful to ask what is going on in their lives; it is possible that they are dealing with challenges that they haven't talked about with anyone else. In Galatians 6:1, Paul doesn't limit this responsibility to elders or preachers (or even youth ministers, for that matter). Paul states that everyone who is spiritual should be concerned for struggling Christians.

James ends his letter by agreeing with Paul – who knows what good could come from you taking action to reach out to your friends?

Putting It All Together

1.   How do you think most of the people you go to school with view prayer?

2.   What is the most challenging aspect of maintaining a solid, consistent prayer life?

3.   Can you think of anyone you know who is a "person of prayer?"

4.   What is your favorite Old Testament story of answered prayer?

5.   Look around. Is there someone in your class who used to be in class all the time but you haven't seen in a while? Maybe you can give that person a call this week and see if you can follow the James 5:19, 20 strategy.

Time-Out #4

Take a few minutes to make a prayer list. You might want to include specific struggles you are facing, blessings in life you have experienced, friends who are sick, or people you know who are struggling spiritually. Take the list with you for your private prayer time at home.

Taking It Home

This week, try keeping up with the prayer list you made earlier. Set aside a specific time to pray each day, and try to keep up with what you pray about through the week. You might even want to take a notebook and make a prayer journal where you write out your prayers. The key is to find a strategy that helps you communicate with God and use it!

Leader's Guide

Teacher Prep For Lesson #1
Before the class...

Put the entire book of James in written form. You can cut and paste from a Bible program or on-line translation, or you can simply type out the entire book. Be sure to take out any chapter or verse numbers (those were put in by human beings anyway) to make it look like an actual letter. Then, mail it to each of your students as if it were an actual letter, and challenge them to read it through before you begin studying it. After you have done that, send them weekly e-mails containing the portion of James you will study for next week (you can even set up a new e-mail account at a free service so that they can get an actual e-mail from "James").

The goal is... to get every student to read the entire book in one setting and think of it like a letter.

For the class session...

Introduction — You can bring a copy of the book *Between a Rock and a Hard Place* to class, or you can download some pictures from Aron's site: www.aralston.com.

Time-out #1 — You might want to do a little research on Hansen's Disease and even bring in a few pictures of people who suffered with it. The Websites for the World Health Organization (www.who.int) and the Center for Disease Control (www.cdc.gov) would be good places to begin.

*The goal is...*to illustrate the importance of pain.

Time-out #2 — Bring in a dumbbell or barbell that is heavy. Try to see how many times you can lift it. It is better for the teacher to lift the weight, since no one needs to be embarrassed in a Bible class (and it is always funnier when the teacher is the object of the joke). If a student volunteers, however, and you think he or she can handle it, let them give it a try. You might also want to bring in a muscular person (one of the high-school football players, for example) to lift it. He or she can explain how lifting a weight like that is only possible for someone who has undergone strenuous workouts.

*The goal is...*to show that strength can only be built by regularly "working out" muscles, causing temporary pain that leads to lasting strength.

Time-out #3 — Be prepared with one or two examples from your own life, in case discussion is slow. Encourage them to be open and share their own thoughts about struggles in their lives.

*The goal is...*to encourage them to think about suffering in a constructive way.

Time-out #4 — Use those Scripture passages, as well as any others you find helpful, to reassure your class that struggling with doubt is normal and God's Word can help them through that struggle.

*The goal is...*The teenage years are full of questions and self-discovery, so it is important for them to realize the solid foundation that God's Word can provide.

Time-out #5 — You may want to provide some of your own visual illusions as well.

*The goal is...*to illustrate the fact that the same events can be interpreted in different ways.

Teacher Prep For Lesson #2
For the class session...

Recap From Last Time — Spend the opening minutes of class asking if anyone kept a list of the challenges faced during an average week. If they are comfortable with it, ask a few to share their lists aloud. Begin with a prayer that God will help them handle those challenges.

Introduction — Many in the class will probably have read this story in school at some point; a few may even remember this particular portion of it. Make sure everyone understands the process by which the raccoon was trapped.

Time-out #1 — Prepare a few Scriptures ahead of time, and begin with those to stimulate thought (Ex. Philippians 4:13, Romans 8:31, etc.) Divide the class into three groups. Ask Group #1 to find passages that remind us to do what is right. Ask Group #2 to search for passages that give us comfort when we feel down. Ask Group #3 to list passages that focus on our eternal destination. Once all groups are done, compare notes and jot down each Scripture.

*The goal is...*to learn Scriptures that will help students handle temptation.

Time-out #2 — Begin by writing on the board the lusts which are mentioned. Remind the students that they are not confessing their lusts; they are merely listing what lusts affect their age group. Then, allow them to draw conclusions about the end result of these lusts. Give them time to think through these answers. It may be a reality check for some!

*The goal is...*to remind everyone of the end result of lust — sin. The better we understand the process, the better we can handle temptation.

Time-out #3 — Ask for two volunteers from the class. Have one of your volunteers step out of the room. While that student is outside, rearrange the chairs in the classroom. Form an obstacle course from one end of the room to the other. Blindfold the volunteer outside, with instructions to cross through the maze from one side of the room to the other. Have every student in class give wrong directions to the blindfolded volunteer. It doesn't matter what directions they give, as long as they are wrong. The end result should be that the blindfolded volunteer is confused and takes a long time to navigate through the maze. (You'll want to watch carefully to make sure that no one gets hurt!)

Now, ask that same person to go through the maze blindfolded, again. Only this time, have the second volunteer stand beside the blindfolded one and give the correct directions in a soft, calm voice while everyone else continues giving the wrong directions. See if the blindfolded volunteer makes it through more quickly.

*The goal is...*to illustrate how much easier life is when we are listening only to God, rather than the numerous voices around us who are sending conflicting messages.

Teacher Prep For Lesson #3
For the class session...

Recap From Last Time — Ask if anyone remembers the process of temptation, and check to see if any students put up a list of Scriptures somewhere in their room/locker, etc. that will help them handle temptation. Remind them that the temptations faced by James' readers are still around today.

Introduction — These figures were taken from the 2003 Gallup Poll "How Are American Christians Living Their Faith?" and the 2000 article "Six in Ten Americans Read Their Bible At Least Occasionally" (both available at www.gallup.com). You may be able to find more recent material to make the same point.

Time-out #1 — Be prepared to share an example or two from your own life to get things moving. If you feel comfortable having a couple of students share their stories, feel free to do so.

*The goal is...*to have each student realize the importance of listening rather than speaking hastily, and hopefully to have some students forgive others and resolve any lingering issues with that person.

Time-out #2 — You might want to do an internet search on Brendon's name and see if you can find a picture or article to show the class.

*The goal is...*to share this memorable story as a physical reminder of how important God's Word is to our lives.

Time-out #3 — You may want to write these on the board or hand a list out to everyone in the class. If possible, bring some of the resources mentioned to class, such as the *One Year Bible*, a set of audio cds of the Bible, or a small notebook that could be used as a study journal.

*The goal is...*to help each student spend more time in God's Word and to get more out of it.

Time-out #4 — Bring a hand-held mirror, and start the exercise with yourself. You may want to read passages about the power of God's Word while the mirror is being passed to each person.

*The goal is...*to allow everyone to focus on improving his or her Christian life.

Teacher Prep For Lesson #4
For the class session...

Recap From Last Time — Begin by asking if anyone tried one of the practices from last week's Time-Out #3 designed to develop better Bible reading habits. If a few are willing, let them share their experiences with the class. Be sure to praise the students who gave it a try and encourage them to keep it up.

Introduction — The opening illustration is designed to put the example James mentioned in the beginning of chapter 2 in perspective. You may want to have your group come up with another example of the same principle. If they do that, you might even ask a few to act it out in front of the class.

Time-out #1 — Hand out some paper, and give a few minutes of quiet time for each student to really reflect on a specific individual that has been treated unfairly.

The goal is... to help each student stop to think about the way others feel and reflecting on how he or she can help.

Time-out #2 — Listen in on the groups as they work and help them stay on track if necessary.

The goal is... to help students realize that God's standards and the world's standards may sometimes collide.

Time-out #3 — It might help to have a few examples prepared beforehand to get discussion going. Luke 5:27-32 and John 4:7-26 are great places to start.

The goal is... to show that Jesus spent a great deal of His time on earth around "unpopular" people. If we are going to follow in His steps, then we will do the same.

Time-out #4 — Write both lists on a board so that everyone can see them, and you might even suggest a few sins and ask the class to pick the list to which it belongs.

The goal is... to emphasize that all sin is falling short of God's law, and that we need to be careful in avoiding all sins.

Teacher Prep For Lesson #5
For the class session...

Recap From Last Time — Begin by asking if the students kept up with the name they wrote down from last week. Did any of them try to reach out to that person? If a few are willing, ask them to share those experiences with the class. Remind those that might not have participated to be on the lookout for people they can encourage at school.

Introduction — The news story that begins the chapter is intended to prompt the class to focus on the tragedy of dead faith. You might want to do a little internet research to print out some pictures that were run in newspapers about the story, or if you find a more current story that gets across the same message, feel free to use it instead.

Time-out #1 — You have probably seen a "trust-fall" exercise before, and the class will likely be familiar with it as well. Make sure you have plenty of participants ready to catch that person; we don't want anyone to get hurt!

*The goal is...*for the students to realize that faith requires trust in something you can't see. If we want to live out our faith, we will have to trust God to take care of us, and it won't always be easy.

Time-out #2 — Familiarize yourself with the Hebrews 11 before this exercise. You might also want to have some suggestions ready for what the students can do to take action on their faith.

*The goal is...*to show that faith has always been more than just mental agreement that God exists — it requires action.

Time-out #3 — Make sure the groups are evenly divided, and encourage creativity. Try to move beyond the commonly given answers. This may be an opportunity to come up with a class service project idea.

*The goal is...*to get them thinking about all the different ways available to use our talents to serve God.

Time-out #4 — This time-out is important, since the discussion of acting on faith is linked to salvation. Some of your students may have questions about becoming a Christian, and it is vital for this class to be a safe place for them to study and discuss that topic. Wouldn't it be wonderful if someone became a Christian during this study?

*The goal is...*to teach the class what faith includes and encourage further study.

Teacher Prep For Lesson #6
For the class session...

Recap From Last Time — Ask the class to suggest some works that they thought of during the week which prove true faith.

Introduction — This story was taken from an article in the October 31, 2007 edition of the *New York Times*. You might also want to bring in a match to give students a perspective of how small it is.

Time-out #1 — You'll need a blindfold and plastic gloves. Once the person is blind-folded, hand them a series of objects. If you have access to a bit for a horse, use it. If you can get your hands on an old steering-wheel (since a ship's rudder might be harder to find), hand that over next. If you haven't used a match already, you can plug that in as one of the items. Now, for the fun part! Hand them a cow tongue you have purchased from a local grocery store. You may need to call ahead, since some stores need advanced notice to order them! If they have gloves on, you can unwrap it and let them touch it directly (or even hold it). Some will think the tongue is incredibly gross, and some will think it is awesome. Either way, it makes a point.

*The goal is...*to make an impression on each student of the different images James uses and to see the connection between those images and the tongue. A tongue outside the body is not that impressive (and maybe even gross), but when it is used, it is powerful.

Time-out #2 — If possible, bring in three sets of paper. First, show them a set of 52 sheets of computer paper, designed to represent all the words spoken in an average day. Then, show them a stack of approximately 364 sheets of paper, to represent all the words spoken in an entire week. The third set should have about 1454 sheets (give or take a few!) to represent all the words spoken in a month. You can ask the class to look at those stacks and imagine all their words for a day, week, or month were contained in them. How much of them are positive, and how much are negative?

*The goal is...*to provide a visual demonstration of how much we talk, and to challenge students to examine the nature of their words.

Time-out #3 — Nothing fancy here, just a practical activity to illustrate the point. You might want to stretch it out a little bit longer, but don't rush it. Let the effect of the silence really sink in to the class.

*The goal is...*to show the class how uncomfortable silence can seem and remind everyone of the importance of quiet time with God.

Time-out #4 — Be prepared with a story of your own, and share what a difference that comment made in your life. This can be a great, uplifting activity for the whole class.

*The goal is...*to illustrate the importance of positive words from a friend.

Teacher Prep For Lesson #7
For the class session...

Recap From Last Time — Start class by asking if anyone noticed a temptation to use their words in a destructive way. Did they hear anyone else use their tongues to tear others down? Share some examples, and then let the class know that this lesson's study of wisdom will help everyone learn how to make better use of their words.

Introduction — The first story is merely an illustration of the importance of wisdom. The two examples are designed to show how everyone makes mistakes; plus, it is easier to laugh at a big corporation that made a mistake than ask students to give examples of mistakes in their lives. You might want to bring in a picture of a Ford Edsel or a "New Coke" can, since they likely won't know about those products. However, they should be interested, since the love teenagers share for cars and soda spans the generations!

Time-out #1 — This one is simple, but you may want to be prepared with a couple of suggestions to get the discussion rolling.

The goal is...to put into perspective how much Solomon gave up in order to gain wisdom. Is wisdom that important to us?

Time-out #2 — Encourage the volunteers to have fun with this — maybe use a goofy voice and say it loudly.

The goal is...to start analyzing actions in terms of worldly wisdom or godly wisdom. The class will practice on these biblical examples, and then they can use that same strategy to examine their own thoughts.

Time-out #3 — Encourage the class not to identify which statement is worldly wisdom and which statement is godly wisdom based solely on which sounds like a "Sunday School" answer. Make sure they are specific, naming certain elements present in each one.

The goal is...to start asking ourselves this question whenever we receive advice or think of an action to take: Does this come from worldly wisdom or godly wisdom?

Time-out #4 — Be familiar with the passage, and remind the class how foolish and shameful the crucifixion would have seemed to the world, even though it is so powerful an event that it shapes our lives as Christians.

The goal is...to remind the class that it does not matter what the world claims as wise; it matters what God tells us is wise.

Teacher Prep For Lesson #8
For the class session...

Recap From Last Time — Ask if anyone was able to carve out time to pray for wisdom over the past few days. Encourage them to continue to make that part of their regular prayer life.

Introduction — Ask if anyone has heard the term "frenemy" before and if they know what it means. Can they think of people at school who have plenty of friends that are sometimes enemies?

Time-out #1 — Make sure that you have the students who are most familiar with Scripture evenly divided in all the groups, so no one who is unfamiliar with the Bible is embarrassed. While the competition aspect shouldn't be emphasized too much, make sure to set a definite time so that you will be able to cover the rest of the passage.

*The goal is...*to show how the warring desires in our hearts can easily lead to sin.

Time-out #2 — This should get them talking! As you guide the discussion, remember to bring up the negative intent associated with coveting — seeing something that belongs to someone else and wanting to do whatever it takes to get it.

The goal is... to make sure the class has an accurate definition of coveting and to remind everyone how the temptation to covet can creep up on us.

Time-out #3 — Make sure your volunteers are good sports, and be sure to explain to the rest of the group how to act around them. Make sure each volunteer has interacted with a few "friends" and a few "enemies" before stopping the exercise.

*The goal is...*to prove how easy it is to see if someone is a friend or an enemy. We can't fool God!

Time-out #4 — You might want to be prepared with some suggestions of your own to get the activity started.

*The goal is...*to encourage the class to remember that God lives in them, and that should affect their actions.

Teacher Prep For Lesson #9
For the class session...

Recap From Last Time — Begin by reminding the class about the difference between being a friend of God and a friend of the world. Ask if they were keeping their eyes open for messages in the media that were anti-God.

Introduction — This story is recorded in several different places. You might want to do a little research on-line, and maybe even come up with a few bull-fighting pictures to share with the class.

Time-out #1 — This is pretty straight-forward, but you might want to come prepared with some examples from your own life to get the conversation flowing.

*The goal is...*to engage the class in honest discussion about the areas of life in which it is difficult to live the Christian life.

Time-out #2 — Make sure that the sticks you bring to class aren't so thin that they will break too easily. Also, it is important to tie them together tightly for the illustration work. Feel free to substitute with other materials, depending on what is available.

*The goal is...*to illustrate how much stronger we are when we have strong Christian friendships.

Time-out #3 — You can judge from the personality of the class how many want to participate. Be sure to ask a lot of processing questions as they go through the exercise — let them describe how it feels to clean people's feet or to have their feet cleaned. Remember, there may be individuals in class who absolutely will not want to do it, and there is no need to force anyone to participate.

*The goal is...*for the class to pause and realize what an act of service foot-washing was in the first century.

Time-out #4 — As you go through this exercise, emphasize that while we shouldn't pass judgments based on our own opinions, it is always necessary for us to compare our lives to God's Word.

*The goal is...*to show the class how vital it is for us to trust God's Word as the only standard.

Teacher Prep For Lesson #10
For the class session...

Recap From Last Time — Ask the group if they noticed who the humble people were in their lives during the previous week. If they are comfortable doing so, let them share the names of those humble individuals with the group.

Introduction — Go over these statistics with the group. If you find more current facts that make the same point, incorporate those as well. Ask the class how their averages line up with those figures.

Time-out #1 — Be sure each person fills out a list, and you may want to provide some time for the students to discuss their goals.

The goal is...to encourage everyone to think seriously about their goals in life and reflect on how those goals line up with God's will.

Time-out #2 — You will want to have all of the supplies in class beforehand. If you are looking for big rocks or gravel, you might want to stop by a construction site and load up a bucket. Make sure you have gone through the illustration before class time so that you have the right amount of each for the object lesson.

The goal is...to illustrate in a powerful way that everything else in our lives is dependent on putting God first.

Time-out #3 — Spray the can a few times so that everyone can see the mist settle into the air.

The goal is...not to depress the group, but to encourage them to act wisely with the life God has given them.

Time-out #4 — Be prepared with some examples of your own, and encourage them to think of real-life situations they might encounter on a daily basis.

The goal is...to remind the group how important it is to follow lessons like this one with action.

Teacher Prep For Lesson #11
For the class session...

Recap From Last Time — You might want to begin by asking if the class thought about life any differently after last week. Did reflecting on the brief nature of our life change the way they acted throughout the week?

Introduction — This might be a good spot to talk about some of the celebrities who are in the news right now. It is frightening to think about how much influence they have over our society, and we need to talk about it with our teenagers.

Time-out #1 — Be prepared with some celebrity suggestions of your own; you might even be able to find one or two who have turned their lives around after getting off track due to stardom.

*The goal is...*not to insult famous actors or musicians, but to honestly assess the lives of the "rich and famous" and see if it is all the media makes it out to be.

Time-out #2 — Have students volunteer to read Scripture, but here is the twist. When the first volunteer raises his/her hand to read a passage, just hand that student a dollar. Don't say anything about it, just make sure everyone can see what you are doing. Then, ask for another volunteer. Hand this one two dollars. After that, take a five dollar bill out of your hand and ask if anyone wants to read the third passage. Before reading the passages, take a minute to discuss how money motivates us.

*The goal is...*to help the class realize how wealth motivates us, and maybe catch them off guard!

Time-out #3 — Ask everyone in both groups to participate in the discussion of how to handle those situations. Try to make sure no one gets left out during that process.

*The goal is...*to allow students to apply scriptural principles to realistic situations.

Time-out #4 — Record brainstorms for both lists, and encourage them to get creative in thinking of ways money can be used to glorify God.

*The goal is...*to have the class imagine the different ways money can glorify God and get specific about ways money can be used sinfully.

Teacher Prep For Lesson #12
For the class session...

Recap From Last Time — Ask if anyone noticed "slander" at school or at their job during the week. If they are willing, let them share with the class how it happened. Were they able to take a stand against it? What are some ways they could handle it in the future?

Introduction — There is a wealth of material on Shackleton and *Endurance* available in biographies, movies, and internet resources. For a good, brief introduction to Shackleton, Leonard Sweet uses the story to illustrate leadership principles in his book *Summoned to Lead.*

Time-out #1 — You can choose whatever plant you like, although if you leave it in the classroom, it will probably need to be one requiring minimal upkeep. It could become a constant reminder of this principle.

The goal is...to drive home the image of a patient farmer and what that means for the way Christians should live.

Time-out #2 — Encourage them to be creative with this one, then drive home the point that we are not promised another day. We need to live every day as if it is the last day we have to work for the Lord.

The goal is...to remind the class that our time on Earth is limited, and it is important how we use it.

Time-out #3 — Although this might work better with a middle school group, even an older class can have fun with it. If you have someone in the class who enjoys making people laugh, you may want to make him Simon.

The goal is...to remind the group how important it is to follow our words with the right actions.

Time-out #4 — You may want to allot a large chunk of time for this activity. Try to split the group so that those who are familiar with the Bible are evenly divided on each team. While this exercise is designed to get students looking through their Bibles, it should not embarrass those who might not be familiar with biblical stories.

The goal is...to have students searching Scripture for other biblical examples they can look to and to show them that the best illustrations for biblical principles are often found in God's Word.

Teacher Prep For Lesson #13
For the class session...

Recap From Last Time — Begin by discussing any biblical examples of perseverance they read about during the week. Ask what specific actions we can take as Christians to develop our perseverance.

Introduction — This would be a good time to talk about how prayer is thought of and talked about by their friends. What do their friends think about prayer? How is prayer talked about in the media? How do those perceptions compare to biblical reality?

Time-out #1 — Have the class think through every aspect of meeting with a famous leader. What thoughts would go through their minds? The more details, the better.

*The goal is...*to gain a deepened appreciation for the awesome privilege of talking to God.

Time-out #2 — Try to select some examples of martyrdom that will really grab the attention of the class. You might want to start with what history tells us about the deaths of the apostles, or you could start with other martyr stories, like Polycarp.

*The goal is...*to put our problems into perspective.

Time-out #3 — Sometimes our prayers are dominated by our own problems or health concerns of our friends. While it is good for us to pray about those things, we don't need to exclude the other aspects of a balanced, healthy prayer life.

*The goal is...*to help the class develop an understanding of all the ways James tells us to pray.

Time-out #4 — While this is a personal activity for each person, be sure to encourage everyone to participate. You may also want to encourage them to develop a prayer journal, mentioned at the end of the chapter.

*The goal is...*to give each class member encouragement to establish and maintain a regular prayer life.

"Andrew Phillips has hit a grand slam with this book! What makes it so good is that it is so practical and well illustrated."

Dr. David Powell
Assistant Dean of Biblical Studies
Freed-Hardeman University

"For decades I have heard youth leaders and teachers lament the scarcity of good Bible school curricula for teenagers. The ones that were biblically responsible seemed to be out of touch with youth culture, and those that were culturally relevant seemed to ignore the biblical text. In *Where Faith Meets Real Life*, Andrew Phillips has demonstrated that it is possible to be *both* biblically responsible *and* culturally relevant. This book is packed full of textual insights, contemporary illustrations, innovative teaching strategies, and windows into the world of today's teenagers. I recommend it highly and believe it sets a new standard for how we teach teens the timeless Word of God."

Bruce McLarty
Vice-President of Spiritual Life
Harding University

"The key to a good Bible class is to make the Scriptures come alive for the student. Here, Andrew makes it easy for us to see just how God's Word can be applied in our everyday lives. These studies are perfect for anyone wanting to see change in their young people and will help show that the book of James is as relevant today as it was the day it was written."

Brad Montague
Freed Hardeman University Staff